The **Paren**alk Guide to Being a Grandparent

The

Parentalk

Guide to

Being a Grandparent

Jim Harding

Series Editor: Steve Chalke

Illustrated by John Byrne

Hodder & Stoughton

LONDON SYDNEY AUCKLAND

Walter de la Mare's poem 'The Cupboard' is reproduced by kind permission of the Literary Trustees of Walter de la Mare, represented by the Society of Authors.

First published in Great Britain in 2002

British Library Cataloguing in Publication Data
A record for this book is available from the British Library

ISBN 0 340 78542 X

Typeset by Avon Dataset Ltd, Bidford-on-Avon, Warks.

Printed and bound in Great Britain by
Clays Ltd, St Ives plc

Hodder and Stoughton
A Division of Hodder Headline Ltd
338 Euston Road
London NW1 3BH

Contents

Acknowledgements

I'd like to thank my Mum for managing to cover three generations as a parent, grandparent and great-grandparent, without
giving up yet. I'd like to thank Sally, my wife, for her patient
encouragement and for being a living example of what a loving
grandparent should be like. I'd also like to thank my three
children, Jamie, Megan and Alice, for what little I know about
being a parent and for pointing out how little that is. A special
thank you to Megan for her help with the typing, which
reduced my number of incidents of computer rage. And, of
course, a big thank you to my four lovely grandchildren,
Christopher, Kelly, Alice and Dan. They are what it is all about.

A thank you to John for the cartoons. (Not all grandparents
have dentures John!) A thank you, too, to Maggie and Tim at
Parentalk for being such good people to work with and for
introducing me to the wonderful world of Top Tips, snappy
headings and the Parentalk way with English literature.

Jim Harding,
York 2001

Introduction

<u>Stepping Out into the Dawn</u>

Of all the relationships open to us, becoming a grandparent is one of the most exciting. Even Mick Jagger is a grandad. Grandparenting must be cool. Becoming a grandparent for the first time is like joining a club. It is not an exclusive club, exactly the opposite. One-third of adults in Britain are grandparents. The club has no rules and the entrance requirement is not even met by us but by our children.

Not all grandparents are happy in their role. Life is not like that. Some suffer acutely as grandparents. Some do not want to be grandparents. Others are unhappy about the way they are treated. A survey conducted for the *Guardian* in December 2000 suggested that almost a quarter of grandparents felt they were being exploited as a source of child care. Another survey conducted in November 2000 found that 70 per cent of grandparents breathe a sigh of relief when their grandchildren are taken off their hands. Some parents long to be grandparents but have no grandchildren; some have grandchildren but never know them; while others know and love their grandchildren but are cut off from them, usually through the parents splitting up. It is the responsibility of the more fortunate of us to remain sensitive to others who have very different experiences.

However, in my experience, the most striking feature of the grandparents' club is how joyful it is. The most common response I get when people discover that I am a grandparent is a smile. Grandparents I know are often happiest when talking about their grandchildren and, viewed from the other side of the relationship, children often brighten up when talking about their grandparents. And I have noticed that, at Christmas, friends who are very shy and who would not normally be seen dead in front of a camera suddenly start sending you cards with smiling photographs of themselves with their grandchildren. Many grandparents would agree with the person who said: 'If I had known what fun grandchildren would be I would have had them first.'

 Top Tip: Grandparents are often surprised by the amount of joy that grandchildren bring.

The Strength in Families

When I retired from my job as Chief Executive of the National Society for the Prevention of Cruelty to Children (NSPCC) in September 2000 I had been working with children and families, in one way or another, for over thirty years. Looking back over that time I am struck by the persistent underestimation of how hard it is to provide loving and consistent care for children outside of their families. Many of the foster-parents and adopters with whom I had the good fortune to work were among the warmest and most generous people I have ever met. I have also been in many good residential establishments staffed by the most dedicated people you will find anywhere. Nevertheless, working first in Social Services and then at the NSPCC, I also saw many awful examples of the terrible damage done to people who suffered abuse and neglect as children in the care system. During the last decade of the twentieth century about 100 care

3

workers were convicted of sexually abusing children in homes around the country and, when I retired, more than 1,000 were still awaiting trial. The North Wales enquiry alone reported that at least 650 children had been abused in children's homes there.

At the same time we have underestimated the love and commitment that can be provided within extended families. Certainly families can be bad for children; I have discovered that often enough. Also families now come in a bewildering array of shapes and sizes. However, within most families there are huge strengths which often remain unrecognised and untapped.

Top Tip: *It's important to recognise and use the strength that families have.*

It is common to hear it said that the extended family has ceased to exist in this country. It is not true. Extended families are alive and well but have taken different forms to match the changes in family life. These changes include the fact that few extended families now live together in closely knit communities (although it is surprising how many grandparents live near at least one of their grandchildren). Because we live longer, and because many children live in reconstituted families, there are more parents, more aunts and uncles, and more grandparents around than ever before.

Grandparents are the most neglected source of strength in families. Much has been written about families and parents but grandparents remain a comparatively neglected subject. It is as if the wolf hid not only Little Red Riding Hood's granny but a multitude of other grandparents as well. Maybe it is because grandparents belong to an older generation that it seems so easy to dump them on the scrapheap. Yet, from the point of view of doing the best for our children, we neglect at our peril the love, care and consistency grandparents can provide.

 Top Tip: *If we want to do the best for our children, we mustn't neglect what all grandparents have to offer.*

Jackie

When I was working in the children's department of an inner London borough at the end of the 1960s I had on my caseload a young couple and their baby whom I will call Jackie. Both the parents were heroin addicts and I became increasingly doubtful about their capacity to care for their baby. Matters came to a head when Jackie was admitted to hospital with serious injuries. There was no doubt the injuries were caused by the parents. I did not believe they had deliberately injured Jackie but could not rule out the possibility of her being hurt again if returned to her parents. Legal proceedings led to Jackie being committed to the care of the local authority.

Jackie was placed, along with dozens of other babies, in a

large nursery. As foster-homes were hard to come by, the next likely step for her would have been a move to a long-term children's home. However, I wondered if Jackie had an extended family and decided to find out. It was not easy. There was little information on file. Because the parents were living a rootless kind of lifestyle it was assumed they were without roots. Also, understandably after what had happened, the parents were reluctant to talk to me as they held me responsible for Jackie being in care. Eventually I was able to find an address, in another part of the country, where the mother had lived before running away to London.

I visited this home and found Jackie's maternal grandparents. They lived in a cosy council house in a poor part of town. They simply could not understand what had happened to their daughter whom they still loved although they had not heard from her since she had run away. They were astonished to hear they were grandparents and distressed to hear their grand-daughter was in care. As I got to know the grandparents better I became convinced that Jackie would have a more loving home with them than anywhere else. The placement was controversial, not least because the grandparents were seen as the very people who had made such a hash of bringing up their own daughter.

I lost contact with Jackie's parents when they moved from their squat but I visited Jackie in her new home with her grandparents a number of times. I do not know the final chapters of her childhood's story but when I last saw Jackie she was doing well at school, had many friends, was happy and had already enjoyed a better start to life than she could have had anywhere else. And all because of the love of a pair of hidden grandparents.

Whatever problems exist in a family, and whatever difficulties grandparents might have in their relationships with their children, they still might have an important part to play with their grandchildren.

 Top Tip: *Grandparents will still have a vital role to play within even the most difficult family relationships.*

Discovering a New World

During my three decades of working with children and families, time and again I had reason to be grateful for the strengths in extended families and the contribution that grandparents could make to the lives of children. But, by the time I retired in September 2000, I had a more personal reason for being interested in grandparents. I had become one. By then I had four wonderful grandchildren of my own.

A new world was opened to me when I became a grandparent. People I barely knew, once they heard I was a grandad, would start telling me stories drawn from their own experiences of grandparenting. Some of those stories I have told again in this book.

But despite all my experience of working with families, nothing had prepared me for the flood of love, pain, joy, apprehension, excitement and pure fun that was to sweep me away as a grandad. Like all close relationships it has its risks.

We cannot love without opening ourselves up to pain. This is what we accept in drawing close to those dearest to us. But the rewards are immense. Everything I learned about grandparents by observation from the outside through my work I now experience in all its intensity from the inside through my family. Both kinds of experience are united in confirming the importance of grandparents for children. Grandparents are good for children; and children are great for grandparents.

Top Tip: *Grandparents are good for grandchildren (and vice versa!).*

'The Linchpin of Family Life'

There are a few signs that this importance might have slowly started to be recognised. The year 2000 saw one of the first grandparenting conferences in Britain. A few books on grandparents have recently been published and the *Guardian* started a monthly grandparents' page at the end of 2000. Launching it Matt Seaton wrote: 'Grandparents have become a social force to be reckoned with.' I hope so.

Harriet Harman, as chairwoman of the Childcare Commission, said: 'Grandparents are the linchpin of family life and insufficiently recognised.' It is time now for that recognition. This book is for all those linchpins, for all kinds of grandparents everywhere.

Throughout the book I have rarely made a distinction

between grandmothers and grandfathers. While they can have different parts to play there are many shared qualities that both grandmothers and grandfathers bring to families. It is on these I have concentrated. I am also concerned about a tendency to air-brush grandfathers out of the family picture (similar comments have been made about fathers). Some books and studies have concentrated exclusively on grandmothers and there is no doubt that grandmothers have a very special place at the heart of society. However, one of the themes of this book is that we should look at family relationships from the point of view of the children and, from their perspective, grandfathers also are important. Another theme is the importance of extended families. Grandfathers too are part of extended families.

 Top Tip: *Grandmothers and grandfathers both have important parts to play.*

Finally, I acknowledge that much I have written about here has been inspired by being a grandfather myself. I want to be true to that experience. It is an experience that was vividly described by Victor Hugo over a hundred years ago: 'Being a grandfather is stepping out into the dawn' (*L'Art d'Etre Grandpère*, 1868).

Top Tip: *Whatever route we travel to becoming a grandparent, doing so opens up a new world of almost limitless possibilities. Grasp the opportunity with both hands and step into the dawn!*

GRANPA, MUM SAYS YOU AND GRANDMA KNOW EVERYTHING...

WELL WE DO... EXCEPT ABOUT GRANDPARENTING.

Grandparents and the Family

The Third Tier

Grandparents are the third tier in a family, two generations removed from their grandchildren. A lot can happen in one generation, let alone two. The nature of families has been changing at great speed. Consequently grandparents are themselves in transition as part of the wider family. They are mixed up in the maelstrom of the debate 'What is the family?'

No Kids Please, We're British . . .

Britain has a reputation for not liking children and for failing to be family-friendly. Many British parents have tales to tell about the warm welcome their children received in cafés and hotels in France, Spain or Italy, in contrast with the cold contempt they receive at similar establishments in their own country. Welcome progress has been made in outlawing prohibitions such as 'No Blacks' or 'No Women', but 'No Children' remains commonplace.

A report 'Is Britain Family Friendly?' by the government-funded National Family and Parenting Institute confirmed this view and denounced Britain as deeply intolerant of both children and parents. Giles Tremlett, writing in _The Times_ (15 January 2001) and living abroad, gave his views of coming to Britain with children: 'It was, as we who visit occasionally can testify, the least child-friendly country in Europe.' In such a scene child-friendly grandparents who love their families can be a great blessing.

It is easy to feel depressed about modern society and to be pessimistic about the state of the family today. However, there is nothing new in the view that the contemporary scene is the worst since history began. L. C. A. Knowles noted that people 'are always despondent about their own times, and it would be easy to quote contemporaries in every period so that their testimony would show that we had gone downhill ever since the time of the Norman Conquest'. Many of us also have highly selective memories when we compare modern times with the past. Something happens to our view of yesterday that makes it seem better than it probably was. I have long-standing friends of my age who complain bitterly about young people, and about how standards have fallen, and yet when I remember us as young people we were every bit as dreadful as we claim are the youth of today. Whatever the truth of the matter there is no doubting that times are different.

Top Tip: *Be tolerant. Every generation has accused the next of falling standards of behaviour, but when we take an honest look at ourselves, we were probably just as bad when we were their age!*

What we as grandparents are most likely to discover is that our children's families are unlike our own. Some of the differences might be unwelcome. Where this is the case we must face our negative feelings and overcome them. If we try to bury them they might not stay down and could erupt in ways that damage our relationships with our children and grandchildren. One way to help with this process of coming to terms with differences is to look into our own history and learn from it. Most of us have a record of changes between generations buried deep within our own lives, especially if we came from traditional families ourselves and were part of the movement towards less traditional ways of family life when we became parents.

Top Tip: *Perfect families do not exist, so face up to any negative feelings you may have and be committed to overcoming them.*

One of the greatest sources of amusement for my children is to take out the photograph albums and look at some of the

pictures taken twenty-five years ago. There to be found are photos of this long-haired, scruffy couple who must be their parents although it is hard for our children to believe it. (Indeed it is hard enough for Sally and me to believe it was us.) Back then, when we were young parents, times were different; now, when we are grandparents, times are different again. Times are always different. Grandparents must adapt. If we can adapt we will have a relevant contribution to make but, if we cannot, we risk being left behind frozen in our one moment of history.

 Top Tip: Don't get caught in a time warp: try to adapt to the special demands of the twenty-first-century family.

Another adjustment we need to make as grandparents is to meet the world as it is. We all have dreams for our children.

14

Sometimes dreams come true but not always. It is essential that we do not let our dreams for the kinds of families we want for our children (married to a handsome prince / beautiful princess, living in a palace, with attractive, bright children arriving at the first attempt and all devoted to their grandparents) get in the way of making the best of reality. There is no such thing as a perfect family because families are composed of human beings. TV advertisements portray a pink and fluffy view of families that does not exist in our everyday world. The advertisements are made to speak to idealistic fantasies within most of us but can leave a feeling of dissatisfaction with the way the world is and with the realities of family life. Our children's families will not be of the pink and fluffy kind, any more than ours were. Indeed, many grandparents will have experienced in their own family lives the problems their children are facing now. Any unrealistic expectations on our part should be squashed for the sake of our children. Our children do not stop needing our love once they become married and have a real family of their own.

 Top Tip: *When they have children of their own, our children need our love just as much as ever.*

Vive la Différence!

People have been grandparents throughout the centuries and have always been important to family life but few

15

generations have had to deal with the speed of change, and the number of challenges, with which contemporary Western culture faces us. In the United Kingdom we live in a mixed community with many different peoples, lifestyles, cultures and religions. Approximately three million people are from ethnic minorities and they may well have different forms of family life. It is important not to try to impose our own view of what a family should look like but to respect, enjoy and learn from this diversity. The modern family is multiform. It does not come in one model but takes many different shapes.

Many of the features of our society, too, can have a major impact on the role of a grandparent. One in three births takes place outside marriage. Many people are staying single after having children with the consequence that children are often now to be found in families with one parent. Single parents represent about a quarter of all families. They might be particularly in need of regular help. Some single parents are permanently on duty with their children and always have to be on

16

their best behaviour. And if they are on their own what happens if they are sick or under the weather? The arrival of a grandparent in such circumstances can be as welcome as the sight of the cavalry emerging from the dust clouds to relieve a besieged fort.

Couples are marrying later than in previous generations, with the current average age being twenty-eight for men and twenty-six for women. Mothers now return to work more often at an earlier stage in their child's life. It has been estimated that both parents go out to work in two-thirds of two-parent families. A provision of substantial child care arrangements is needed to support both parents in work. It is often grandparents who step in to meet this need.

 Top Tip: With changing family patterns, grandparents are needed more than ever.

The UK also has the highest rate of teenage pregnancies in Europe. Very young parents may be particularly in need of the experience and support of their own parents.

The family of today is becoming more fluid and more fractured. The UK has one of the highest divorce rates in Europe. Forty per cent of marriages will break up if the current trend continues. Many people, after divorce, will enter a new relationship and this will mean new relationships too for children. Sometimes when parents are involved in a number of relationships children inherit an impressive array of relatives including a battery of grandparents. These changes result in kaleidoscopic shifts in the patterns of families.

When Your Family Grows Overnight

Grandparents may find themselves with step-grandchildren when a new family forms. I first became a grandparent when my son married my daughter-in-law who had been married before with two children by her first marriage. I suddenly found myself a grandfather to two children aged six and four (they are now my adopted grandchildren). It was one of the most exhilarating times in my life. The first task was to learn the language. My grandchildren had been born and brought up in Gateshead and spoke Geordie. There was a major communication gap between us. My son helped by giving me a book called *Larn Yersel Geordie* and by offering me much encouragement of the 'ganonkidda-getstuckin' kind. I slowly came to realise that a phrase like 'Yerg'annies cowped her creels' means 'Your grandmother has stumbled'.

Some grandparents might have mixed feelings about 'inheriting' step-grandchildren. It is important in these circumstances for grandparents to be honest with themselves. Any ambivalence should be identified and tackled. It might not be as easy as it sounds but it is a necessary step if a grandparent is to concentrate on the needs of their new step-family and avoid acting out any unresolved emotional problems of their own. Being a step-grandparent is different from being a 'biological' grandparent. The new relationship between step-grandparent and step-grandchild often has no history. Consequently it takes

18

time to develop trust, affection and understanding. This requires patience and consistency. Too much should not be expected too soon. It helps to see the relationship from the child's point of view. These new step-grandparents might be the last kind of addition to their family the children would have chosen, if they were in a position to choose. It is understandable if step-grandchildren are guarded at first. It will take time for them to feel safe and happy in their new family. However, and this is my experience, there is no reason why a step-grandparent and step-grandchild relationship cannot gradually grow to be as close and as loving as any grandparent–grandchild relationship.

 Top Tip: *It takes times to build up a relationship with your step-grandchild so don't expect too much too soon.*

It is also important to be sensitive to members in the wider family, some of whom might be dropping out of the picture as you come in. Children and grandchildren are likely to have strong feelings about these changes. Jealousy and rivalry between the members of a family under these circumstances are not uncommon but will only make the children's lives miserable and will make it difficult for them to come to terms with what has happened. Wherever we are coming from within the family, our loyalty should be to the children. It is their needs that should be met.

> **Top Tip:** *Regardless of what is going on within the wider family, the needs of the children should always come first.*

Breaking Up

One of the hardest blows for grandparents to bear strikes when changes in the family threaten to cut them off from their grandchildren, especially if their son or daughter is the parent without custody. Many parents, when they separate, are very skilful and caring in managing the break-up of their relationship in a way that most helps their children. Often the children maintain a loving relationship, and regular contact, with the parent who leaves home and with other close relatives. Parents and grandparents are usually on the same side in striving for what is best for the children.

However, unhappily for the children, it does not always work out peacefully like this. At the NSPCC I saw many cases of violent disagreements between separating parents and their respective families over the care of the children, and witnessed the chronic effects these family wars had on children. Some of the angriest, and most threatening, letters I saw were from aggrieved relatives, often grandparents, caught up in these disputes. It was common for allegations to be made that a disliked parent, or new step-parent, was physically or sexually abusing their children. While sometimes these accusations were well founded, far too often they were simply a way of trying to hurt a parent they disliked or a ploy to get custody of the children.

In dealing with breakdowns within the family we must give far more consideration to the needs of the children. They have emotional lives too. It is all too easy to dismiss consideration of the children with the convenient assumption that they are resilient and will bounce back soon enough. Nor should they be treated as ammunition to be fired at the other side in a dispute. We will all have seen examples of children being deliberately hurt in order to get back at somebody else. Although it is a risky enterprise grandparents can act as protectors for children and stand between warring partners to insist that children are treated as precious individuals with needs of their own.

 Top Tip: *Children are easy to use as ammunition. Grandparents can play a key role as protectors for children whose parents are warring.*

An Anchor in the Storm

Arrangements following family breakdown that are entirely practical, and do not take into account the emotional life of a child, are hurtful and damaging. When statements are made such as 'You must take her, it's your turn this weekend' or 'I had to have him last Christmas, you have him this year', the child has become little more than a shuttlecock to be knocked

21

between opposing players. It is a cruel irony that while this is happening there might be grandparents in the background longing to spend time with the child.

The wider consideration of the needs of children should take in a broad sweep of relationships that are significant to them. No one who is important to a child should be written off. Too often members of the extended family are not taken into account. Grandparents can be very important to children in helping them to deal with shifts in the family, particularly if they involve bitterness and ill feeling. Grandparents can provide a safe place for children to shelter in while the family storms rage outside. They can also offer the crucial comfort of continuity. In times of upheaval we all find it helpful if we can cling to somebody who offers reassurance that our whole world is not falling apart.

 Top Tip: *Grandparents can offer a safe haven to grandchildren who may be feeling that their world is being turned upside down.*

Grandparents can help in yet another way. If their parents stop loving one another, children can fear that love will stop for them too. As grandparents we can make sure our grandchildren know that our love for them is unqualified and enduring. When parents do break up it often happens that children blame themselves. It is as if they think there must be something wrong in them that has caused all the unhappiness. They desperately need help in understanding that the problems of the parents are not the responsibility of the children. They are not the cause of the pain. By reassuring their grandchildren that the breakdown is not their fault, and by showing them how much they are still loved, grandparents can help prevent children shining the beam of blame onto themselves and help to protect their vulnerable self-esteem.

Top Tip: When families break up, grandparents can reassure children it's not their fault.

The significance of grandparents rests in the good they can do for their grandchildren. Few would disagree that it can be tragic when, in family breakdowns, children lose their grandparents and become 'grandorphans'. However, grandchildren are not the possessions of their grandparents. Although it is a sentiment often expressed by grandparents, I do not believe we have a right to our grandchildren. They are not here to provide us with comfort and company. It is the other way round. Children should have relationships with their grandparents in order to help children to be loved, valued and able to fulfil their potential in life. It is children who should have a right to this kind of relationship.

Top Tip: Children have a right to loving grandparents, not vice versa.

Not Taking Sides

Grandparents caught up in family conflicts will need a big heart. We will need much good judgement and, often, not a little courage. But if we can avoid being blindly partisan, or totally identified with one side of a feud – even if it involves our own child as one of the parents – then we can be in a central position to help our grandchildren. Grandparents can be close enough to understand what is going on, yet sufficiently distant from the pain and intimacy of the conflict to keep an eye on the interests of the grandchildren. This may require a very delicate approach. As parents we will want to support our child while, as grandparents, we will want to support our grandchildren. If there is conflict between those two aims

YOUR GRANDPARENTS WILL BE SOLID ROCKS OF SUPPORT TO YOU WHATEVER HAPPENS...

GRANDPA CERTAINLY WILL BE... I'VE JUST MIXED CEMENT WITH HIS DENTURE FIXATIVE!

managing both can be hard. Whatever the circumstances, however, it never requires a withdrawal of love. It is possible for us to love our own child unreservedly while battling for the best for our grandchildren. Grandparents can be the grandchildren's champion. We can be the guardian watching over our grandchildren's wellbeing and ensuring their best interests are always the paramount consideration.

Very occasionally, grandparents may find themselves in a complex family situation where, however caring and conscientious they might be, their continuing involvement cannot be in the best interests of their grandchildren. This might be particularly true where a family has been reconstituted many times with grandparents accumulating at a bewildering rate for the children involved. In these painful circumstances it may be necessary for grandparents to make the ultimate, loving sacrifice of their own relationship with their grandchildren.

 Top Tip: *In any situation, always looking out for the best interests of the child will help any grandparent to know how to respond.*

Fortunately, such instances are rare. Usually the needs of children and the love and experience of grandparents are in such harmony that the relationship is mutually rewarding and precious.

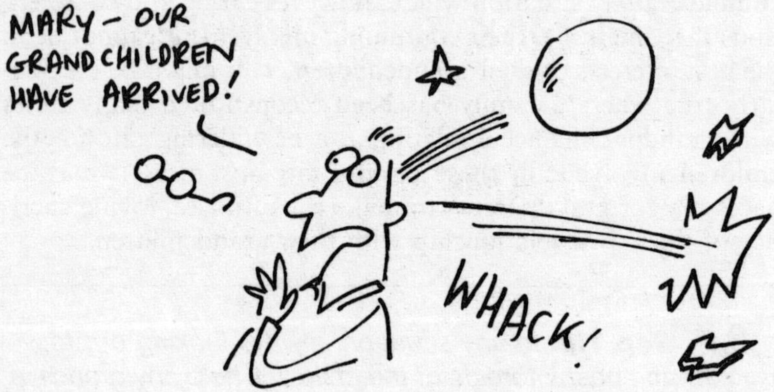
MARY - OUR
GRANDCHILDREN
HAVE ARRIVED!
WHACK!

Becoming a Grandparent

A Time for New Life

The Birth of a New Generation

Every time a baby is born, a parent and child are pushed forward a generation, a child becomes a parent and a parent becomes a grandparent. But it is not only at the birth of a child that people become grandparents. A broad range of paths lead to this position. It could be through becoming a step-grandparent, through adoption or fostering, through legal arrangements or through caring arrangements outside the immediate family circle.

And just as there are many routes to grandparenthood, we will have many different reactions to becoming grandparents. Most of us approach it as a knight in the Middle Ages might have approached the Holy Grail. Research in the USA has suggested that as many as 96 per cent of adults wanted to become grandparents. Indeed I expect many of us know parents who are so keen to become grandparents that they put pressure on their children to have children of their own. Understandable as it may be, it is wrong and unhelpful to try to force our children to fulfil our wishes. It is their decision whether, or when, to have children, not ours.

Top Tip: *Parents do not have a right to become grandparents. It is for our children to decide if, and when, they want to be parents.*

Easy as ABC?

In any case, conception itself is not always straightforward. In some parts of the Western world it has been estimated that one in six couples is unable to conceive at all. Many others have to wait a long time. A parent obviously impatient to become a grandparent can, if they're not careful, only add to the pain. In such circumstances our children require sensitivity from us as well as our unqualified love and support for them in their own right – whether they become parents or not.

Top Tip: *Our children need our love and support, regardless of whether or not they become parents.*

When It's Not the Best News that You've Heard All Day

For other soon-to-be-grandparents, the news of their new role is greeted with less enthusiasm. Unlike some cultures we have no rite of passage to help us into this new stage of our lives. There are many reasons why people may be unhappy about being grandparents. If we find it hard to face the fact of our ageing we might take this to the extreme of not wanting to be grandparents for fear it will make us seem old. Or we simply may not take to the role of grandparent, perhaps because we cannot be in charge in the same way as we were as parents. People may also feel that they have done their stint, as parents, in bringing up their own children and may want to enjoy a freedom from family commitments when their children grow up. This might be particularly the case if a parent has postponed a career, or a special interest, or ambition, while the children were at home. When children become independent, parents have another opportunity to ask what they want to do with their lives. The answer might not always accommodate grandchildren.

Sometimes the problem can be simply a matter of timing. People might become grandparents at a time of hardship in their own lives because of, for example, redundancy, illness or bereavement. In such circumstances a time of healing might be needed before moving into the new relationship.

In other circumstances, the route to becoming a grandparent can be a problem in itself. For example, one woman, who described herself as 'pretty traditional', had a lesbian daughter who was artificially impregnated. The 'expectant' grandmother was desperately worried about what kind of relationship she could have with a child conceived, in her view, in such a strange way. When homosexual men have children, grandparents come onto the scene by a route which is often alien to an older generation. Similarly, a good friend of mine very much wanted a child but she had been unable to form a permanent relationship with anyone. In the end she set out deliberately to become a single parent. She became a devoted mother but discovered that her parents always found her chosen lifestyle difficult to accept.

Worth it in the End

Whatever route we travel on our journey to becoming a grandparent – whether rough or smooth, short or long – waiting at the end of the road is a precious relationship, a relationship between grandparent and grandchild; a relationship crossing generations; a relationship full of potential. It is tragic if people who can be, and want to be, active grandparents cannot reach this relationship either because of problems of their own or because of disapproval of their children's behaviour. It may require considerable strength to remove the barriers and overcome the obstacles. Healing, forgiveness and acceptance may all be needed but the reward of making a contribution to the life of a grandchild is worth fighting for. It need not require abandoning a moral position, or compromising our values, because our grandchildren are not responsible for the way they burst into our lives.

 Top Tip: It may take time, tolerance and forgiveness, but your relationship with your grandchild is worth fighting for.

A New Start

For some, the birth of a grandchild sows the seeds of reconciliation. Parents and children sometimes become estranged. If the damage to the relationship is not repaired, not only will a child

lose parents but, when that child in turn becomes a parent, a grandchild will lose grandparents too. After the breakdown of a relationship, however remote the possibility of parents and children getting together again may seem, it is always worth seeing the birth of a grandchild as an opportunity to change things for the better. Sometimes these little bundles of new life can achieve the seemingly impossible and bring healing to long-standing injuries. Both sides of the damaged relationship have the chance to resolve outstanding problems from the past so that they can face together, in a fresh way, the future that is embodied in the grandchild. One grandparent said: 'The birth of my grandson was highly significant. For two years I had been estranged from my son but when the baby came along he said that he did not want to deprive his son of a grandmother. It was as if there was a crack in the door (the barrier) that was between us. Now my son and I have established a new relationship. In a way my grandson salvaged our relationship' (quoted in Jean King's *Never Mind the Gap*).

Top Tip: *The birth of a grandchild can help to heal a broken relationship.*

When I look at my two children who now have families of their own, I marvel at the new people they have become. As grandparents, we can have a new understanding of our children as they enter parenthood. It is a view that usually brings respect, admiration and a renewal of the love we have for our children at the deepest level.

From the other point of view, children often look on their parents with fresh eyes after having children of their own. They can now share the common language of parenthood. At this time it is common to hear comments like: 'Now I know what you had to put up with!' 'How did you cope without a washing-machine?' 'Only now, trying to be a good mum myself, do I realise what a good mum you were to me.'

The arrival of a grandchild is a momentous occasion for both the parent and grandparent and a wonderful opportunity for creating a new relationship with each other. It is the golden age of forgiveness.

Top Tip: *The arrival of a grandchild provides the opportunity for both grandparent and parent to reassess their relationship.*

Walking with Dinosaurs

As we enter the territory of grandparenthood, however, there can be the occasional unwanted label or reaction that accompanies our new status. We cease to be the last generation and become the one before that, vanishing into the outer regions of prehistory to be the human equivalent of a megalithic stone circle. We become part of the grey brigade, whatever our age. We are called 'old fogeys'.

One of my closest friends is a retired architect. He is also an accomplished painter. Through a shared interest in painting he established an e-mail relationship with an Italian webmaster he had never met. There was a lively and regular correspondence over many months about art and life in general. Then my friend received the following communication: 'Now I need to tell you a bit about myself. I'm twenty-nine with a girlfriend older than myself and she has a young child. But this relationship is not very easy because my parents still don't accept her. Well, what about you?' My friend replied that he was a grandfather with two children and two grandchildren and the communications came to an abrupt end. He never heard from his 29-year-old Italian webmaster again.

Similarly, a grandfather was once asked by his daughter, 'Why don't people over fifty have children anymore?' When the grandfather said he did not know his daughter continued, 'Because they would put them down and forget where they left them.' Now it is true that grandparents can belong to that generation where we are always forgetting names and can never remember where we have left our specs but, at the same time, we are relied upon not to forget when the grandchildren are coming to stay, when we are due to baby-sit or the dates of our grandchildren's birthdays!

These reactions and responses should not bother us as grandparents because they can be turned on their head. For the truth is that becoming a grandparent is often a time of renewal and rejuvenation. Our life is given new meaning. It is a time when the number of our close relationships expands and when we have the joy of being with children once more. Seeing the world through the eyes of children puts us back in touch with that innocent zest for life which, however deeply interred, remains within all of us. Vanessa Ball wrote about grandchildren: 'What a blessing they exist . . . and what an incredible difference such small creatures make to life. They're so full of it, it seems to spill over all around.'

 Top Tip: *You may be called an 'old fogey', but becoming a grandparent will give you a new lease of life!*

Getting Ready

Becoming a grandparent is one of the most monumental landmarks in our lives. Can we prepare for it? We have already noted that there is no rite of passage for grandparents-to-be. Our society does not recognise grandparents in any special way, as some cultures do. For example, in Japan (although it is beginning to change now) grandmothers have traditionally been permitted to wear the colour red as a badge of their status. Living in the UK, grandparents-to-be can expect no externally awarded special privileges but this does not prevent them from working out their own way to prepare for being a grandparent.

It is unlikely that grandparents-to-be will find prenatal classes, or a course to attend, although such opportunities are beginning to be developed. Instead grandparents will need to prepare themselves and it might be helpful to give attention to a number of points in advance.

1 Review Our Own Experience

Nearly all of us will have had grandparents of our own. My paternal grandfather died before I was born and my maternal grandmother died when I was young. I have a few memories of my paternal grandmother. She ran a sweet shop and visiting her should have been a dream come true for a little boy, but she was stern and odd and I was always a little afraid of her. Once, when I stayed with her overnight, she threw out the two soft toys I loved and slept with. She considered I was too old for such comforts and would 'grow up to be a sissy'. It was my first experience of bereavement and I never forgave her. It taught me to respect the early attachments of young children, whether it be to a soft toy, a blanket or some other object. When our children have kids of their own, we can revisit the relationships we had with our own grandparents and decide what was good and bad about them. We can be determined to build on the good elements and avoid the bad ones.

> ***Top Tip:*** *By revisiting the relationships that we shared with our grandparents, we can build positive foundations for the future with our grandchildren.*

Bad experiences can be overcome and even helpful in giving us guidance about what to change. A 52-year-old grandmother – I will call her Mary – hated her own grandmother who could not stand having Mary near her because she was such a noisy child. This left Mary afraid she would be the same as her grandmother. Nevertheless when the time came Mary was a loving and effective granny. Her positive grandparenting was a deliberate act to correct and counterbalance her childhood experience of what grandparents were like.

By contrast we are likely to have good memories too. I was an only child, and often lonely, so it was always a joy when my maternal grandfather came to stay. I called him 'Gramps', which is the name some of my grandchildren now use for me. What I liked about him especially was that I never had to be on my best behaviour with him. Rather the opposite! We were often like two impish children relishing our naughtiness. We had to share a bedroom and long after I was supposed to be asleep we talked while Gramps smoked his illicit cigars, tipping his ash into an empty peppermint tin, and drank from a bottle of rum he kept hidden under the bed.

I liked him, too, because he was funny and we laughed a lot together. He told me many stories. I am not sure how true they were, but I expect he did fight in the Battle of the Somme as a young recruit who had been inspired by the rhetoric of Lloyd George.

Gramps was Welsh. I loved his accent and some of the strange Welsh words he used, particularly when he was swearing. He came from a remote village in central Wales but moved to South Wales to get work. He worked down the coal mines until he contracted silicosis and then worked as a commercial traveller, going up and down the Rhondda valley before retiring. His memories were my family history.

Gramps always persuaded himself to get up with exactly the same words every morning: 'Well, as my old mother used to say, this and worse will never do, this and better may do.' One of my most precious possessions is an old fob watch he left me.

I would like a bit of Gramps to live on in me as a grandfather.

 Top Tip: *You'll be amazed at how, just by spending time with them, you can build memories that your grandchild will treasure for a lifetime.*

---

2 Remember Our Own Childhood

Another way we can prepare for grandparenthood is to remember our own childhood and those of our children. Contained in these memories will be a rich store of inspiration about children we can draw on as grandparents. I am surprised how easily we forget what we were like as children. This can be most evident when we sit in judgement on today's children as if we were always clean, tidy, polite, considerate and obedient children ourselves. Some hope!

Top Tip: *Remembering what we were like as children can help us to be better grandparents to our grandchildren.*

Remembering what children are like will prompt us to look afresh at our own homes, gardens and treasured possessions. There is little point to complaining about a smashed valuable vase if we left it on a knee-high stand when a toddler visited. We need to protect our treasures but we also need to ensure our homes and gardens are safe places for grandchildren. This child-proofing check will require compromise but we can make our home safe and, at the same time, an exciting place for grandchildren to visit and explore. I know grandparents who set aside special cupboards, drawers and desks for their grandchildren to delve into. Although they contained ordinary, everyday objects such as lids, buttons, pans, boxes, paper and pencils they were an endless source of enjoyment. Their existence also made it possible for the grandchildren to be redirected there from no-go areas.

We cannot have our cake and eat it. We cannot have the pleasure of our homes exactly as we like them and, at the same time, enjoy the pleasure of visits from our grandchildren, at least when they are young. My daughter called my grandson, when he was a one-year-old, 'the benign destroyer'. When he came through the front door it was like letting in a whirlwind. After only a short visit to our house it was amazing the trail of debris this little body could leave behind. Yet he is a cheerful character and the chaos he caused was not the result of ill-disciplined behaviour but of tremendous energy linked to a huge interest in the world.

 Top Tip: *Children are human dynamos. Accidents will happen, so if you want to protect your treasures, think carefully about child-proofing your home.*

We have friends who live in a lovely, beautifully furnished house full of antiques. They love their grandchildren but go through agonies whenever they visit. Our friends spend all the time rushing ahead of their grandchildren trying to anticipate their next moves in order to prevent the next disaster. As a result the grandchildren's visits are tense and unhappy. A comparatively minor change to the layout of the house, and a few special arrangements for the children, could make these visits far more relaxed and fun for everyone. The trouble is as we get older we tend to become more rigid and more resistant to change. For some of us the interiors of our homes might just as well be set in concrete. Our grandchildren will help us to ease up if we can be flexible enough to overcome our set ways. In doing so they will introduce a more dynamic quality to our lives and free us from our self-built tombs. New grandchildren bring new adventures.

3 Talking to Our Child

In preparing to become a grandparent it is important to talk to our child who is preparing to become a parent. It can be a joint preparation. The BT advertisements insisted it's good to talk. So it is but so often we don't. I cannot claim that I ever sat down with my children and talked about becoming parents and grandparents but, with hindsight, I wish I had. Most of our talking has taken place as we have gone along but much could have been done in advance.

Talking about becoming grandparents with our partners and our children is a way of thinking and feeling ourselves into the role. This is much easier to achieve in conversation with others than it is in trying to puzzle it out on our own. As we talk, we will start to open the exciting range of possibilities and opportunities that lie ahead. In these conversations it is likely that differences in views and approaches will crop up. To be able to identify and talk through these early on is a great help. Also we will have opened up a channel of communication that can be used in the future without embarrassment or awkwardness.

 Top Tip: *Talk to those close to you, especially your children, about what it means to be a grandparent and their expectations of you.*

This process of sharing the anticipation of the new world ahead will underline that becoming a grandparent is about two relationships, not one. It involves not only the grandparent's relationship with their grandchild but also the relationship with their own child. There is something miraculous about the transformation when your child becomes a parent. You are now both parents. The grandparent is a parent of a parent.

In becoming a grandparent it is important we recognise that in the matter of bringing up grandchildren our children are the bosses. It is a radical turnaround, with the children confirming their independence by becoming the new parents and the older generation becoming dependent, to some extent, on the wishes and needs of their children. This is not to say that grandparents should not offer advice or speak out from their own experience. Many parents are only too pleased to have good advice and to benefit from the experience of others. But, when it comes to the crunch, unless some special arrangements are in force, it is the parents who are in charge.

 Top Tip: *Remember – your child is the boss when it comes to bringing up your grandchildren.*

If grandparents simply do their own thing, or insist they know best, it will not only undermine the parents but will also confuse the grandchildren. Children need consistency. More than that, they thrive on it. It can only be disturbing to a child if the adults they love treat them very differently and behave in incompatible ways. If we find ourselves slipping into this type

of behaviour, we need to work hard to agree with our children a common approach. This does not need to result in some bland uniformity – after all part of the value for grandchildren is having close relationships with different kinds of people – but it must lead to consistency in such matters as discipline, diet, values and the way children are allowed to spend their time.

Top Tip: *Grandchildren need consistency to thrive. Support your children as parents in the values and standards of discipline that they want to set.*

Alternative approaches to parenting adopted by our children can be a bitter pill for us to swallow if we see any differences as a criticism of our own parenting skills. We all want to be good parents and to provide good role models for our children when they become parents. But, despite what we're sometimes led to believe, the perfect parent has yet to step out on this earth. It is natural our children should want to put right anything they found unhelpful in their own childhood. (After all, isn't this exactly what grandparents did in their own past, when they became parents?) And besides, every parent will have a unique personality and will bring something especially theirs into their relationship with children.

 Top Tip: *The perfect plan for parenting does not exist, so be ready for your child to adopt different approaches to parenthood.*

Offering Support

Support is an important issue today because there seems to be an epidemic of low confidence, with many parents suffering from severe doubts about their parenting skills. An industry of books, guides, classes and counsellors has sprung up to support parents. While I was working for the NSPCC I was often asked to appear on television, or speak on the radio, in order to offer advice to parents. Doubts about whether I was qualified to give any advice at all came to me when I returned home from one such appearance to find my children helpless with laughter. They were astonished to discover that this very fallible and everyday person they knew as their father could have the nerve to advise other people on how to be a good parent.

 Top Tip: *At a time when parents are often lacking in confidence, one of the best contributions a grandparent can give is to support their child in the decisions they make.*

The strongest source of support for parents is from their own parents. In *The Parentalk Guide to the Childhood Years*, Steve Chalke makes the point that 'Your child needs your unconditional love to survive and thrive in life'. This need does not suddenly get turned off when children grow up and it can become a major need again at the dawn of parenthood. Grandparents can do so much to help their children believe in their ability to be good parents. After a visit of our two grandchildren ended in a fight, followed by a deafening, joint screaming fit, my daughter was embarrassed and concerned and started to question her ability to be a good mother. As she left I gave her a hug and said that, as far as I was concerned, she was a wonderful mum. She is too, but appreciated the encouragement. Kind words soften hard times.

Top Tip: *Even after becoming a parent, your child never stops needing your unconditional love and support. Be prepared to put it into words.*

Grandparents can also offer much reassurance based on their own experience. They have been through it and have earned the life-as-a-parent T-shirt. Parents can believe they are uniquely awful in some way. Grandparents can often reduce these fears by simply pointing out that many child-rearing problems are common and to be expected. Observations like 'That often happens at this stage', or 'It won't always be like this', or even 'You were even worse at that age' can come as a great relief. Grandparents can bring problems down to earth, such as those with sleeping, feeding, learning, behaviour and relationships, and make the commonplace normal. Just as our children, when they were young, needed to hear us say, 'I love you', so, many years later, they may need to hear us say, 'I love you and I think you're a great parent.'

 Top Tip: *Grandparents can reassure their children that the problems that they are facing with their own children are not necessarily new and can be overcome.*

Becoming a grandparent will be a different kind of experience for different people but I know many will share my sense of wonder and awe when the time arrives. Grandchildren are a blessing and becoming a grandparent is one of life's miraculous moments, like falling in love or the birth of your first child. It is a time for new life.

The Part Grandparents Can Play

A Mutual Bond

Although the word 'grandparent' is easy to define in terms of family relationships there are as many different kinds of grandparents as there are people who are grandparents. There is no blueprint for being a grandparent, any more than there are set rules for other kinds of relationship. Every grandparent is an unique individual with their own particular contribution to make. Striving to be some kind of ideal grandparent will only undermine the natural contribution we can make as ourselves. The advice to be true to yourself holds good for grandparents. It is essential in relationships with children who seem to have X-ray vision that can identify phoniness and pretence.

Top Tip: *Whatever you may want to be, as a grandparent always be yourself!*

We're Getting On a Bit . . .

Grandparents come from different backgrounds, cultures, religions, races and places. They can be anything from thirty to 110 years of age with the average age of becoming a grandparent being fifty. As people live longer a larger proportion of their life is likely to be in the grandparent years. In 1901, 4.5 per cent of the population in the UK were over sixty-five and 0.2 per cent over eighty-five. By 1997, 13.9 per cent were over sixty-five and 1.8 per cent over eighty-five. The forecast for 2021 is that 16.9 per cent of the population will be over sixty-five and 2.3 per cent over eighty-five (*Annual Abstract of Statistics*, 1999). In 1970, according to the Institute of Actuaries, a sixty-year-old man could expect to live until the age of seventy-eight; by the end of the century he could expect to reach eighty-four.

Top Tip: *With people living longer, many of us will be grandparents for a significant proportion of our lives. To make the most of our lives, we'll need to make the most of being a grandparent.*

It is taking us a long time as a nation to adjust to changes in the weighting of our lives. Families are expanding vertically. Becoming a grandparent is now more likely to occur nearer the middle of our lives than the end. We have to ensure we make the very best of these changing patterns of ageing in our own lives. And what is true for us as individuals is true for us as a nation. Unless we make the best of the potential offered by grandparents, the waste will be mountainous.

Many of us are retiring earlier. According to the Audit Commission, the average age for the retirement of council employees, for example, is fifty-four. Only one teacher in five now continues working until sixty-five. Consequently the time we have is not only lengthening but also emptying. Grand-parents can be the beneficiaries here. With more time, and fewer demands being placed upon us, we have more opportunity to invest in our grandchildren.

> **Top Tip:** Early retirement provides a great opportunity to invest in your grandchildren.

... But Have So Much to Give

These sociological changes, however, do not always go hand in hand with an awareness of the fantastic human resource that older people can be. Rather the opposite. There are some good signs, of course, which indicate that society may be waking up to the untapped potential of the older generation. For example, so-called 'Silver Surfers' are now recognised as significant contributors to the enormous growth in the use of the Internet over recent years. Similarly, there are now organisations that specialise in linking up retired professionals with voluntary organisations keen to make the most of their experience and expertise. But despite these small pinpricks of light, ageism still rears its head as a very common prejudice in our contemporary society. Older people are often stereotyped as weak and sick and a burden on the fit and healthy. I often hear people referred to as being 'past their sell-by date'. Thus are human beings reduced to has-beens and unwanted objects. An editorial in the *Spectator* (30 September 2000) described the 'ever-increasing burden that the elderly are placing upon the young', especially with regard to taxation.

If we are ever to appreciate fully the ongoing contribution of older generations, our picture of maturity needs to be repainted representing its colour, its vivacity and its richness. One of the most potent ways of achieving this is through recognising and celebrating the contribution grandparents make. They can be of service to the young rather than a burden to them. Children who have warm, loving relationships with their grandparents see them as dear and precious friends and not as worn-out mounds of wrinkled flesh outliving their usefulness. Thus are stereotypes broken down and destroyed.

The Roles that Grandparents Can Play

There are many, many roles that grandparents can play. We can be playmates. This is when we are discovered happily lining up the toy soldiers to catch the toy train to travel to the toy school, on the track we put together, unaware our grandchild fell asleep ten minutes ago. We can be heroes, courageously hunting down and driving out the dragon and the wild things from the nettles at the bottom of the garden. We can be living ancestors and family historians, making our grandchildren dizzy with disbelief by showing them photographs of ourselves as babies and therefore younger then than they are now. Or we can be chauffeurs, finding out that buggies are prepared to collapse only if they can crush your fingers and that children's car seats can be fitted only by rocket scientists.

Top Tip: *When you become a grandparent you may well discover hidden talents that even you didn't know you had!*

We've also been called all manner of things from 'mother's helpers' or 'cost-free childminders' to 'surrogate parents'. The range of contributions grandparents can make is enormous. Even in terms of direct care this can move from occasional carers to regular baby-sitters, to day care grandparents, to living-with grandparents and on to custodial guardians. The following brief descriptions are not exhaustive, nor should they imply that the roles come in watertight compartments. They overlap one another all the time. However, the list could be useful in helping us to understand what kind of grandparents we want to be and what we want to offer. Talking to our children about our own hopes and expectations can help to ensure that we offer the children as consistent, and as varied, an experience as possible. Grandchildren, as they grow older, will soon have views of their own about what kind of grandparents they want and what they want to do with us. We should always be ready to talk about this vital area so that we do not impose what we want on our grandchildren but remain sensitive to their wishes and needs.

Top Tip: *Talk to your children about your hopes and expectations of being a grandparent.*

The help that grandparents can offer includes the following:

1 Continuous Care

Continuous care can take the form of day care or caring for grandchildren for a longer period. There is evidence that nearly half of all daily child care is provided by grandparents. A *Guardian* poll suggested that over a third of British grandparents work the equivalent of a three-day week looking after grandchildren. This care is invaluable and 40 per cent of parents claimed their working lives would be impossible without the child care provided by grandparents.

Many grandparents enjoy the time they get to spend alone with their grandchildren, but this is not always the case. There is growing evidence that some feel that they are being taken advantage of and being used because of the lack of other forms of care. There may not be easy ways of resolving this, given grandparents' natural wish to support their children and to be available for their grandchildren. Bearing in mind the enormous resource that grandparents provide, I believe the Government should consider offering grandparents financial recompense for this level of care. To do anything else increases the likelihood that we could be left as 'forgotten carers', providing indispensable services for children on the cheap.

When grandparents provide vital but informal child care, the most important thing to do is to ensure that arrangements are kept constantly under review. This is the only way to prevent minor problems from festering into resentment. Problems that remain unaddressed can contaminate relationships and, at the very least, damage the quality of the care our grand-children receive.

 Top Tip: *If you help to care for your grandchild on a regular basis, never shy away from talking to your children about any potential problems that the arrangements create.*

The longer, and more regular, the periods of care the more crucial it becomes to make sure that grandparents and parents are being consistent in the care they are providing. The harder, too, grandparents will have to work at keeping their relationship with their grandchildren special in some way. Perhaps William Hazlitt was being unduly pessimistic when he wrote 'though familiarity may not breed contempt, it takes the edge off admiration', but the observation is sufficiently true to put us on guard to make sure that demanding care arrangements do not take the edge off what we can offer our grandchildren.

The closer the grandparent becomes to being a parental figure the more the kind of advice often given to parents becomes relevant to the grandparent. We need to know, too, that it is all right to feel tired, that it is natural to feel fed up and put out at times. Also, in passing our grandchildren back to their parents, we should not feel guilty if we're overwhelmed by a sense of relief. This is not a sign of a failure, nor a lack of love, but simply relief!

> **Top Tip:** *It's only natural to feel a sense of relief when, after a hard day, you pass your grandchildren back to their parents!*

2 Baby-sitting

Age Concern has estimated that thirteen million hours of baby-sitting is done each year by grandparents. At the level of a minimum wage this would cost parents millions of pounds a year. If there is a substantial distance between homes, baby-sitting may involve an overnight stay or a longer period of care.

I WOULDN'T MIND BABYSITTING IF THE BABY WOULD ACTUALLY SIT ONCE IN A WHILE!

Any parent will readily testify to the value of an occasional break. A night out, a visit to friends, a short holiday or simply a time together for Mum and Dad can make a huge difference. Being a parent is the most demanding job in the world but there are no statutory holidays. If they live nearby, grandparents can help parents to have time for themselves by baby-sitting. In doing so not only will they be helping directly through building up their relationship with their grandchildren, but also they will be helping indirectly by giving their children an opportunity to recharge their parenting batteries.

Grandparents may need to take the initiative in suggesting a break, or a rest, and in offering to baby-sit. Some parents are reluctant to ask for help. At other times they might have become so stuck in the day-to-day slog that it does not occur to them to make a break. Approaching grandparents will always be easier if they are known to be keen to help and to enjoy looking after their grandchildren.

 Top Tip: *By offering to baby-sit, grandparents can throw a lifeline to wilting parents who need a break.*

3 Support in a Crisis

All families have crises. They may be caused by accidents, breakdowns in relationships, loss, illness, death and natural or unnatural disasters. They can involve the whole family or strike a particular member of the family, parent or child. Crises can be sudden and are unsettling and unnerving. For children in troubled times, and indeed for their parents, the best friends are those they know and trust. Enter grandparent! For many children, grandparents are the rocks that have stayed steady at times of upheaval. They have been the fixed stars in the sky above an exploding world.

Top Tip: *In times of trouble, grandparents can be a huge and constant source of strength.*

In addition to the big issues that can hit us between the eyes, there are those silly, niggling, little things that can also cause us so much grief. Whether it's the children's repeated ear infections, the unsuitable friend, the capacity to manage on two hours' sleep a night, or the peculiar dress sense, it is often comparatively minor life events that cause the most anxiety. With these humdrum horrors it is ghastly to have someone around who is censorious and specialises in wisdom of the pull-yourself-together sort. It is much better to have a friend who understands that the size of a problem is often defined by the way we feel about it, and who is simply prepared to listen and to be what help they can. If grandparents know their children well they will have this kind of understanding.

 Top Tip: *Be prepared to help your children with life's niggling little problems as well.*

I loved the childhoods of my children but I have to admit that, when they were younger, one such niggling thing for me was the trial of the birthday party. I remember one where all the children decided to be pigs. They made a rattling good job of it. Food was soon plastered all over the walls. I was so pleased my mum was on hand to help us navigate our way through the chaos!

While I was writing this chapter my youngest granddaughter had her fourth birthday party. It was a case of all hands on deck. My wife and I helped with the preparations, the party itself and the clearing up. Just as my mum had helped us out all those years before, we were glad, in our turn, to offer support to our own kids as they faced the preschool onslaught. It was a very happy party but, afterwards, all the adults involved were exhausted and eagerly looking forward to a fortifying drink. Remembering our own children's parties made it a special pleasure to be able to help with the parties of the next generation. Grandparents should have willing hands.

 Top Tip: Your children will appreciate all the help that you can give them, as long as you avoid the temptation to take control.

Most grandparents want to help in a crisis, big or small. But do our children and grandchildren know this? Perhaps we assume they do, but it is much safer to tell them directly. How often do we find ourselves saying words like, 'I wish you'd told me. If only I'd known I could have helped'? In fact, we should make it our business to know and try to make it easy for our families to talk to us.

Top Tip: *Regularly tell your children that you're available, and willing, to help them – don't just assume that they already know.*

All good relationships work in two directions. Relationships that are all give and no take, or the other way round, lack depth. Grandparents in a crisis themselves might get great comfort from their grandchildren. It is very rare that a grandchild cannot touch a grandparent's heart. In his classic novel, *The Pickwick Papers*, Charles Dickens details the response of one particular grandfather to the attention of a grandchild:

> A young girl – his little granddaughter – was hanging about him: endeavouring, with a thousand childish devices, to engage his attention; but the old man neither saw nor heard her. The voice that had been music to him, and the eyes that had been light, fell coldly on his senses.

Fortunately few of us will ever reach such a position but, in lesser ways, we must be careful never to reject or ignore our grandchildren's loving childish devices. They are the greatest gifts we will ever receive. Simone de Beauvoir wrote: 'The warmest and happiest feelings that old people experience are those which have to do with their grandchildren.'

Top Tip: Make the most of the time your grand-child wants to be with you – it won't last forever!

4 Being a Teacher and Mentor

Grandparents can be teachers without trying. An American study reported that children learned from their grandparents in an effortless way; through 'osmosis' in the words of one of the children. The ease of this process may be due to most children, particularly older children, feeling no need to oppose their grandparents' influence as they might do with their parents in the process of becoming independent. Grandparents are encyclopaedias of the past, capable of providing information from their own lives that children are unlikely to learn anywhere else. For example, a grandad might remember when you could buy a good pint of bitter for one shilling and sixpence and explain that this is what we call seven and a half pence today. Just one word of caution here – although we may see ourselves as a never-ending fount of highly amusing anecdotes and illuminating trivia, we should be prepared for some of our memories and stories to be better received than others. The boundary between being a fascinating history teacher and a boring old fart can be very thin. But, if we pay attention to the views of our grandchildren, they will let us know what goes down well and when.

Top Tip: *Listening to your children will help you to know what stories go down well.*

Grandparents are great for stimulating their grandchildren's imaginations. This can be achieved through games, shared activities, recollections and stories. When children describe their grandparents they talk about doing everyday things together, about laughing and playing. With a grandparent, learning is not only natural, it can also be fun.

Top Tip: *Grandchildren can have great fun learning with their grandparents.*

Some grandparents may be reluctant to take on the role of teacher, perhaps out of humility or because the word 'teaching' – from their own experiences of formal education – invokes negative feelings. It's important to overcome such feelings because grandparents can offer so much as a natural part of their relationship with their grandchildren and without the need for formality.

And it's not a one-way street. We will often find ourselves learning from our grandchildren. Those of us with young grandchildren can see with new eyes the wonders of the world. Things we have taken for granted for years become new and fresh. We may realise for the first time that a soft toy is really a fierce tiger; that trees and flowers blossom; that a walk to the

shops is an adventure; and that an electric guitar is actually a musical instrument! With older grandchildren we can rediscover the mental agility needed to engage in challenging arguments. The learning process for the grandchildren is just as much a relearning process for the grandparents.

Top Tip: As grandparents we can learn just as much – sometimes more – from our grandchildren as they learn from us!

5 Spiritual Guidance

Spiritual guidance would once have been a straightforward part of the relationship between grandparent and grandchild but it is a tricky matter these days. We have become cautious and suspicious about spiritual pronouncements. The positive side to this is that it reflects a greater tolerance and sensitivity towards people with different values and faiths; the worrying side is that it might make us reluctant, or unable, to talk about our own convictions and beliefs. When with their grandparent a grandchild needs a relationship with a whole person. The better the relationship the more complete the giving to each other becomes. Our spiritual side is a vital part of us. If we try to deny it, or repress it, we will diminish ourselves and harm what we have to offer.

 Top Tip: *Your spiritual side is a vital part of you, so it's better to be open and honest about your convictions and beliefs.*

Grandparents are understandably wary about imposing their beliefs and values on their grandchildren. However, sharing something is not the same as imposing it. If we are proud of our beliefs and values, if they are important to us, if they have given us encouragement and helped to guide us through life, of course we will want to share them. In any case if most grandchildren are like mine you will not be able to avoid this issue. My young granddaughter has a rich vein of questions in the what-is-the-meaning-of-life style where it is impossible to respond honestly without stepping into spiritual waters. Even the where-do-things-come-from questions involve getting your feet wet. My older grandchildren ask the bluntest questions in the most unembarrassed way: 'Do you believe in God?'; 'Why do you go to church?' (or 'Why don't you?'); 'Is sex before marriage wrong?'; 'Is divorce wrong?'; 'Is abortion?'; 'Is cloning?' And if you get away with a superficial answer at the start there are all those 'why?' questions waiting to take you into deeper seas.

Children have active spiritual lives. They are bombarded every day from all sides with values and beliefs, and exhortations to do this or to do that, to buy this or to buy that. Television, the Internet, advertisements, comics, pop music and peers are all pumping out value-laden messages. The world is clamouring all the time for access to the minds of our grandchildren.

 Top Tip: *If you don't share your own values and beliefs with your grandchildren, you can be certain that somebody else will share theirs!*

Grandchildren are far more likely to be brainwashed by the hard-selling pressures of modern society than they are by grandparents. In such an environment caring grandparents will, and should, want to make a contribution. The values of grandparents, because they belong to an earlier generation, can be of particular importance in helping children to develop a critical approach to contemporary culture. This will give children the confidence to make their own decisions, to work out for themselves what to accept and what to reject, rather than being carried away on the tide. This is the road to wisdom. It is the way leading to the capacity to distinguish between the right and the wrong, the light and the dark, the profound and the superficial. Grandparents are faithful companions accompanying their grandchildren on the winding road of personal growth.

 Top Tip: *A grandparent is in a great position to help their grandchild develop the confidence to make their own decisions.*

We need not use force and coercion – grandchildren will make up their own minds when they grow up. At the end of the day they will be more influenced by deeds than words. To have pious views that are contradicted by actions is to live as a hypocrite. We should not advise grandchildren to do one thing while we do another. For example, we should not tell them to be honest and then lie to them. The advice, 'Do as I say and

67

not as I do' is the route to zero influence. We have to be open and sincere with our grandchildren, and to be seen to be striving to live according to the beliefs and values we profess. It is what we do, more than what we say, that will play a part in the spiritual development of our grandchildren.

Top Tip: *You're a role model – like it or not!*

6 Being a 'Support' Parent

The rather vague description ' "support" parent' is intended to describe the very special response of a grandparent to a very special need. Examples of such needs would be if a grandchild has a disability or serious medical condition, or if parents become critically ill or are injured. I have not covered this in detail because the role is not a general one but is adapted to particular circumstances and might require specialised skills and knowledge. Nevertheless we should honour the part that grandparents play in offering this kind of help. At almost any point grandparents might make all the difference to a family when special needs arise.

Long-distance Grandparents

Most of the roles described previously require grandparents to live reasonably close to their grandchildren. This will not be true for many people. They may live at the other end of the country or in a different country altogether. This need not destroy the relationship between grandparent and grandchild; close relationships can transcend geographical separation, but it will change their nature.

> **Top Tip:** *Even at a distance, you can still be a great grandparent.*

A loving relationship can be conducted at a distance but it will require a little thought and ingenuity. Means of communication become all important. Letters and phone calls are likely to be popular. These can be used at obvious times; for example, a card and letter, and a long-distance telephone call, might help to make a birthday a very special occasion. However, they might be useful at other times too. One grandfather described an urgent need for contact when his grandchild was born hundreds of miles away. He asked his daughter to bring her baby to the telephone so he could hear the noises the baby made.

Modern technology can help. E-mails, the World Wide Web, video conferencing, fax machines and other developments could all have a part to play. As well as the transmission of the written and spoken word, it is now possible to meet and see each other across large distances. Grandchildren might not only see their distant grandparents in photographs but meet them on videos.

> **Top Tip:** *Advances in technology will help you make the world a much smaller place.*

Distance can be turned into an advantage. It can open up for grandchildren a curiosity for another part of the country, or in another country, broadening their area of interest. Also having grandparents in, for example, Australia, Austria or America, might be good for their street cred. And with visits to distant grandparents, infrequency is going to be counterbalanced by these trips being very special kinds of adventures when they happen.

A Mutual Bond

Whatever parts grandparents play they are likely to be very important ones. Research has shown that for children 'the grandparent–grandchild bond was second in importance only to the parent–child bond'. It is a beautifully mutual bond. Grandparents can add so much, so naturally, to the lives of their grandchildren and the grandchildren, for sure, will do the same for us.

Grandparents and Young Grandchildren

Great Playmates

Alice's Game

In the first June of the new millennium I was called upon to do some serious grandparenting. My granddaughter, Alice Charlotte, three years old, went into hospital for what was supposed to be a short exploratory operation. Instead of a minor procedure Alice was in the theatre for over four hours. In the waiting-room my daughter and son-in-law were strung out in time wondering what was happening. We all know these unexpected, fearful crises when everything turns cold and the heartbeat of the world seems to stop. After enough time had passed to imagine every possible disaster the surgeon appeared. All was explained. During the operation a polyp the size of a walnut had been discovered and the decision was made to remove it immediately. The operation had been successful and there were no complications. Further tests would be required but the surgeon was reassuring and confident that Alice would not need further treatment.

Nevertheless she had to stay in hospital overnight. Megan, my daughter, stayed with Alice. That evening I drove to the hospital some distance away. I took with me a suitcase packed with necessities for Megan by my son-in-law. He had to stay at home to look after his son, my grandson, Dan aged eleven months.

When I arrived at the hospital it took me over half-an-hour to find out where to go because Alice was booked in as a day patient. It was late, the shops were closed and the place was eerily empty and quiet. It was with relief that I found the bright lights of the night ward. And then, suddenly, I saw them both; my daughter and granddaughter. I was struck with two immediate emotions. The first was an admiring love for my daughter, smiling, serene and totally absorbed in the welfare of her child. The second was a painful love for my granddaughter, bewildered and sad. She was only three years old yet here she was strung up and attached to all the wonders of modern medicine. After giving me a brief welcome Alice held up her arm, with its tapes and drips and tubes, and made it clear that I was nearly as much to blame for this sorry state of affairs as her mother.

The next morning we heard the good news that Alice could go home. My son-in-law prepared to go and collect his wife and daughter. Sally, my wife, was in the final rehearsals for the York mystery plays so it was my task to look after Dan in my home. To be honest I faced the prospect with mixed emotions. I was happy to be able to help, and excited, but also apprehensive. Although a veteran of changing nappies thirty years earlier, I had not remained in practice and the contemporary equipment of disposable nappies looked distinctly unfamiliar. I could not see how they would readily drop into a bucket of Napisan! Also I was afraid that Dan, although he knew me reasonably well, would not accept me on my own. I had seen him when he was displeased and it was not a pretty sight!

In the event Dan was a star. He crawled over the house revealing nooks and crannies I never knew existed. I found myself at floor level, crawling along behind, and seeing the world through new eyes. Our two cats decided on discretion and fled via the cat-flap through which, later, Dan helpfully posted a few precious belongings into the rain outside.

After two hours I was beginning to feel a little weary. Fortunately Dan was showing signs of wear and tear as well. I switched on the sport on television and sat down with Dan in my arms. One minute he was full of life and wide awake, the next he was flat out and fast asleep. I made myself comfortable on the sofa, soothed by Dan's warmth on my chest, and settled down to watch *Football Focus* and enjoy a time of peace.

Then, damn me, with the difficult bit done, there was a knock on the front door. There smiling on the doorstep were my daughter and son-in-law with Alice, who was understandably grumpy. Having gone twenty-four hours without food she was desperate to go home for a big breakfast. On seeing his mum again my charge, Dan, had a spasm of leg-kicking ecstasy and leaped into her arms. They left together, a happy, reunited family.

Football Focus was an anti-climax after all that.

However that was not quite the end of the story. The next morning my daughter, son-in-law and two grandchildren came round to see my wife and me. Dan showed no sign of even recognising me. Alice, however, led me firmly into the garden. It was a clear, sunny day. She ordered everyone else away. Her parents, brother and grandmother were dismissed and ordered not to watch. Whatever was about to happen was strictly between Alice and me.

She made me spread out on the lawn the tatty pink blanket we used for picnics. The blanket was to mark the limits of the world Alice was about to create. Toys and various bits and pieces were collected as Alice introduced toy soldiers, dolls, building bricks, marbles, toy animals and a variety of other objects into this new world. I sat at one end of the blanket, Alice at the other. Every toy and object was transported, one at a time, by boat, plane and then train, first to the doctor and then to the hospital. When they came out of the hospital Alice and I agreed they were happy and had been made better. After that, one at a time, they all came to visit me at the other side of the blanket. I had to pretend to open the door with a special key and let them into my imaginary house. There each visitor was given a huge breakfast before leaving, fully restored and replete, for the grass beyond the blanket. It took about three-quarters of an hour to complete the game. Then, having acted out her own trip to hospital, Alice abruptly got up and joined the others indoors. I was left to tidy up the toys, fold up the blanket and follow on behind.

Alice had moved on but I was in no doubt that something important had happened. The game will soon be forgotten by Alice but I will remember it as a time of intense sharing, when something as precious as peace of mind was reached with the help of a band of toy soldiers, dolls, building bricks, marbles, toy animals and a pink blanket.

oOo

Many of the qualities required of a grandparent do not change with time. Grandchildren, whatever their age, benefit from the love, the example, the interest and the understanding of their grandparents. Other aspects of being a grandparent change depending on the age of the grandchild. This chapter concentrates on the relationship between grandparents and young

75

grandchildren with, as illustrated by the world of Alice's pink blanket, a special emphasis on the importance of play.

The New Baby

Books on parenting often start with the arrival of the baby but the cycle of creation begins long before then. There is time to be spent trying for a baby (possibly experiencing the sorrow of miscarriages) and then being pregnant, or going through the procedures for adoption. Becoming a parent is one of the most common human experiences but it is neither sudden nor simple; it can be planned or unplanned. Parents-to-be may need considerable support through a pregnancy, particularly if it is the first.

This should also be a time of preparation. Babies are wonderful but they are hard, dirty work and demand a lot of time. I have known many parents who simply had not appreciated what a difference a baby would make to their lives. One of the most common factors associated with child abuse is parents' unreasonable expectations of their child. Parents who cannot accept the limitations imposed on their lifestyles, or the demands made of them, have a tendency to take it out on the children. Parenthood is the most important job of all but one for which there is no training, no supervision and little preparation. Helping with the preparation for parenthood can be the first task of the grandparent-to-be. They have been through the process themselves and can offer information and advice from their own experience. They are in a good position to establish a sharing relationship with the expectant parents because they will be going through a simultaneous process of transformation; moving from being a parent of a child to a parent of a parent. At the same time their child moves from being a child of a parent to a parent of a child. This is a time for looking forward. The foundations of the grandparent–parent–grandchild relationships can be laid down well before the birth of the baby.

> **Top Tip:** *Your first job as a grandparent-to-be may well be to help your child get ready for parenthood.*

One difficulty we all face when we talk about babies is that it is the one age for which we cannot draw on our own experience. Babyhood is before memories. We can only guess what it must have been like having the tiger of hunger gnawing at our insides and not to be able to speak out, or to feel the sharp pain of a freezing wind on our faces and not to be able to tell anyone. No wonder babies cry. A curtain of oblivion hangs in our mind and hides those first years from our memory. It is a curtain that can only ever be opened in a very limited way. When parents look at their baby they see a time of life that is a blank to them. The mental cupboard of recollections and experiences is bare. When grandparents look at their baby grandchild they can remember when they first looked on their own child and call upon their earliest experiences of parenthood. This is one of the reasons why grandparents can be so important in the early years of a child's life.

Experts are agreed that our experiences at the start of childhood are critically important in shaping the rest of our lives. It is during this time that our emotional attitude to the world develops. Will we see it as dangerous and hostile? Or as welcoming and friendly? The answers may lie in our earliest experiences of life. Studies (and sometimes our own experiences) show that babies who do not know love, and are deprived of love's physical expression in hugs, kisses, cuddles and caresses, can suffer permanent emotional damage. There is nothing so important to a young child as the certainty of being loved.

 Top Tip: Nothing is so important to a young child as the certainty of being loved.

The infant is at the mercy of the world. After love, the first great needs are food at regular intervals, care for bodily comfort and cleanliness, and protection from danger. If these are available the child is off to a good start. Parents are the source of this care and nurture for their children. They know how to provide this partly by inborn instinct and intuition, partly by their practical intelligence and ingenuity, partly through the advice of doctors and child experts, but also through the example and traditional wisdom handed down by grandparents, especially grandmothers.

When a grandchild is born grandparents will already have made a contribution through their example of parenting. However, this is also a time for advice and practical help. The birth of a new baby is the most wonderful occasion but it can also be an immensely stressful time, especially if it is a first child. It is at this time that it is important for grandparents to strike a balance between involvement and interference. We need to know the difference between the two. The birth of a baby is often a time when greater involvement is needed, but it should not take a form that interferes with the natural development of the bond between parent and child. This is no less true as the child grows up.

 Top Tip: *Know the difference between involvement and interference.*

I can remember how relieved my wife and I were to discover that we were not the only parents in the world to have as our first baby a character who needed very little sleep – unlike us! We thought we must be doing something wrong. Ever since then, whenever I hear anyone say happily 'I slept like a baby',

I know they have never had one. It is all too easy for parents to blame themselves when difficulties occur with babies and young children. Grandparents can insist that much that happens is not a sign of failure but is par for the parental course. Some babies don't sleep much, some eat fussily and messily, some cry a lot and some are experts at high-speed, long-distance throwing up.

Although babies are cuddly bundles of dependency, the state of babyhood should never be glamorised to the point where we feel guilty if our response is anything but awe and wonder. All babies are ghastly gushers of gunge at one end and show a total lack of responsibility at the other. Help with the mucky tasks, as well as the cuddly ones, is help indeed. No one is more likely to do this for a hard-pressed parent than a grandparent.

 Top Tip: *Grandparents are there to help with the mucky tasks as well as the glamorous ones!*

Unhappily, it is not uncommon for a mother to suffer from some form of depression after the birth of her child. This can take many forms, from 'baby blues' to full-blown clinical depression. The cultural expectation that this should be a time of joy can make the condition one that does not attract sympathy or understanding, even though the victim is more aware of this contrast than anyone. When depression strikes it might well be a grandparent who is the most acceptable person to assist with a non-judgemental and uncensorious concern for the mother while, at the same time, standing in for her to help with the care of the baby.

> **Top Tip:** *Your understanding and persevering love will be invaluable if postnatal depression strikes.*

Life with a Storm Trooper

In my experience one of the high points of parental stress occurs when a child is a toddler. It is then that sharp, precious and breakable objects in the house need to be moved up a few feet or moved out. It is the age when the stiffly arched back is perfected making it impossible to get the little darling in or out of a buggy or a car. It is also when a child discovers the word 'no' and explores its meaning to the limit. This is the period when discipline becomes firmly established and boundaries are set. But such advances cannot be achieved overnight. Not all children are the same but most will go through a time of trial and testing out. These are the forgotten years and even people who were parents themselves can conveniently forget what they were like in order to be able to indulge in a self-righteous sniff of disgust. What is hurtful to a parent with a storm-trooper toddler is to be refused an understanding hand of help and offered instead a superior look of disapproval.

Top Tip: *When you have a toddler in tow a helping hand will be more appreciated than a disapproving look.*

Shopping with Megan

I remember (oh, how well I remember!) taking my two-year-old daughter round a crowded supermarket to do the family shop. My daughter saw a large bar of chocolate and insisted on me buying it for her. I refused in a firm but loving way. But 'no' was not then an acceptable answer to my daughter. She asked again. I refused again but explained why and tried to divert her attention elsewhere. After a short whimper my daughter decided that direct action was needed to express her disapproval and started to take things off the shelves and throw them on the floor. As soon as I could pick them up and replace them she had moved on to the next shelf.

When she saw how agitated I was becoming she knew she had hit the jackpot. Her campaign was brought to a towering climax when she removed the very bottom, toddler-high can in a tall pile of cans. The whole lot came crashing down. Amid an ocean of dented, rolling cans I made my feelings clearly known to my daughter who promptly threw herself on the floor and screamed. While a shop assistant picked up the cans I tried to pick up my daughter. No way! She had learnt the stiffly arched back, which made her bend in a way that defied elevation. I left her on the floor, considered giving her a little kick (I hadn't started work with the NSPCC then!) but thought better of it. Instead, I walked away, confident that the sight of me leaving would bring her to her senses. Oh foolish man! It did nothing but increase the volume of the screams.

I returned defeated and would have done anything to pacify my daughter. I would even have bought a hundred large chocolate bars but it was too late now. My daughter was choking on her screams and was so red in the face she looked as if she might explode at any minute.

Amazingly, in this busy supermarket, everybody got on with their shopping as if nothing was happening, simply taking care to steer their trolleys safely around the two-year-old lump of noise on the floor. No one spoke to me. Then, at last, appearing like an apparition in the mists of despair, I saw a little grey-haired woman walking towards me. She had a kind face and looked like everybody's favourite granny. She stopped and looked at me; she looked down at my howling daughter, and then she looked at me again and uttered the immortal words, 'If that was my child she wouldn't be allowed to behave like that', before walking away.

The behaviour of toddlers is so often interpreted as a failure of the parents to impose discipline and exercise proper control. This is usually not the case. It is the point in development when a young child is beginning to understand the nature of discipline and to accept the boundaries being established but has not yet achieved this. It is the age when very strict parents can have very wild children.

Top Tip: *Remember – all toddlers push the boundaries.*

Grandparents are people who remember. They will recall what toddlers can be like. They are the custodians of the normal and the reliable voice about what is acceptable and what is to be expected. This is a prime time for grandparents to cultivate the habit of biting our tongues. Phrases like 'I wouldn't have done it like that' can undermine still further a wobbly parent and should be buttoned up. Words of encouragement are needed instead to fortify your child's self-confidence. Parents need to be reassured that their toddlers are not pint-sized Al Capones with no future other than as drug-dealers and gunrunners.

Top Tip: *As parents of a toddler, your children will need your reassurance more than ever!*

Sometimes a good laugh can help. After all toddlers, in much of what they do and the responses they get, are very funny. It might be the right time for a grandparent to share with a harassed parent a few stories about what they were like at their toddler's age. My daughter was very relieved that my granddaughter, as an active and demanding two-year-old, did not pull off a scene quite as dramatic as the one my daughter had managed in the supermarket over twenty years before.

Top Tip: *For the stressed-out parent of a toddler, having a grandparent on hand to laugh with can be a healthy way to let off steam!*

In Their Own Good Time

Children will grow and develop at different speeds and in different ways. *Vive la différence!* That is part of their uniqueness and what makes them special. However, the achievement of the developmental milestones by young children is in danger of becoming an obsession. Time and time again I hear parents say, in a way that sounds unmistakably like a boast, that their child was by a remarkably young age potty-trained, walking, counting to a thousand, reading Dickens and solving the *Times*' crossword. Reaching a milestone early is seen as a sign of superiority, an accomplishment worthy of attracting the world's admiration. The parental proclamation is not issued as an act of thanksgiving (which can be done in the quiet of a grateful heart) but as self-congratulation and a type of developmental 'keeping up with the Joneses'.

Of course all loving parents will want their children to achieve their full potential but the competitiveness that is dragged into child development meets mostly the needs of the parents, not of the children. Unless there is a particular reason why not, children will arrive at the landmarks in their childhood when they are good and ready. Janus Korczak – a heroic doctor who ran homes for children in the Warsaw ghetto, and who was one of the best writers about children I have read – wrote: 'What is the proper time for a child to start walking? When she does. When should his teeth start cutting? When they do . . .'

In this race of growing up, it is easy to be insensitive to the feelings of parents whose children might be developing more slowly. Grandparents, standing outside the competitiveness, can point out that children develop in different ways. They can champion their grandchildren's progress and make sure that what is normal is not allowed to become a crisis. They can reassure the parent that it is perfectly all right for children to start to walk, or speak, or read, in their own time.

Top Tip: *Avoid getting caught up in competition about the speed of child development. Reassure your children that their own children will develop in their own good time.*

On the other hand, grandparents, with their own experience of children, may also be able to spot when something might really be wrong with a child. It is possible that a parent, wanting everything to go well for their child, might find it difficult to face up to a problem and do nothing, hoping it will simply go away. In these situations a brave and sensitive grandparent can offer advice in a loving and gentle way. Grandparents can then stand by the parent and grandchild offering practical and emotional support as the problem is faced and dealt with. If problems prove to be long-standing, a good grandparent hangs in there and does not give up or go away.

Communication

Good communication is essential for the sustenance of all relationships. As young children struggle with words, and deal with the challenge of expressing themselves, they will need encouragement. It is all too easy to dismiss their first attempts as nothing but baby talk. Talking to oneself, or chatting to a closed mind, are unrewarding activities. A child who is ignored may be reluctant to try talking again. To be effective communication needs a response. If you send out a SOS signal you

SHE SAID ANOTHER NEW WORD TODAY — ONE I HAVEN'T HEARD SINCE I WAS IN THE ARMY.

desperately want to know if it has been heard and understood. Some of the first messages attempted by children are like SOS signals saying something like, 'Hey, you out there, I want to talk to you, do you understand this?'

Young children's early attempts at communication should be a cause of delight, rather than dismissed for being too limited and considered unworthy of an adult's attention. The thinking of a child is not inferior to that of an adult. It is different. A child tends to think with feelings rather than the intellect. That is why communication is complicated and speaking with young children is a challenging art.

 Top Tip: *Children need to be listened to – paying attention will build their self-esteem and encourage them to communicate more.*

Even very young children communicate. A baby's cry is the first human act of communication and a baby soon learns to read a parent's face as a farmer reads the sky. Later a child communicates in the language of gesture and thinks in the language of images. My grandson, when he stretches out his hands towards a desired object, accompanies the gesture with an urgent sound something like 'eh-eh-eh'. It is a little like the alarm call of a blackbird. The sounds means 'Give it!' He keeps reaching out and, when he finally succeeds in getting the object, his face lights up and he sighs as if saying, 'At last!' Now if I try and take the object away from him he will have dozens of different ways of saying, 'Not on your life, I'm not giving it

88

up.' Then, gradually, he might trust me enough to give it to me on the strict understanding that I return it to him immediately and thus the notions of giving and taking get communicated. And, while all this is going on, what do his bright eyes, gurgles and smiles communicate if not: 'I'm happy to be alive'?

When grandparents approach their grandchildren they are likely to have two feelings: affection for the child today and respect for what they can become. Grandparents are less likely to write off the early offerings of sounds from their grandchildren perhaps because many of us are reaching the age when we have started to lose, and forget, words and names and consequently no longer take them for granted. It is a joy to witness the birth of words and to know they will grow into the vocabulary of an adult person. I have watched in amazement as language has come to my young grandchildren. It is a time of laughs and surprises. I could not begin to explain why my grandson started with a first phrase, rather than a first word, nor why that phrase should be 'Shut the door.' However I can guess why his word for cats is 'Gone' because ours usually have, straight out of the cat-flap, when he storms into the house.

 Top Tip: *Grandparents have the experience to enjoy, and assist, their grandchild's language development.*

Grandparents, being older and more aware of the limits to their wisdom, are often more ready to admit they do not know everything. They will not be expected to have the answers in the same way parents are. There are no quick answers to such questions as 'Where did the world come from?' or 'Where do we go when we sleep?' or 'Why do noses stick out?' A busy parent may answer without thinking too much in order to get on with other things. A grandparent may be able to spend time with their grandchildren wondering about such questions in mutual bafflement. These conversations are the child's first expeditions into the deeper regions of the mind.

The Importance of Play

Another crucial area of early child development where grandparents can make a major contribution is play. Play is often misunderstood. It can be seen as simply messing about. For adults the word 'play' is often used as the opposite to 'work', as in the saying, 'All work and no play makes Jack a dull boy'. This distinction does not apply to young children. Play, it has been said, is the child's work. Apart from being a way of having fun, and testing out one's brain and limbs, play is the child's route to finding out about the world. Knowledge starts in play.

For example, the ubiquitous game of peek-a-boo helps a child understand that objects and people can reappear and come back after they have vanished from sight. This realisation is essential to the growth of trust. Hide and seek, in which a child enjoys the thrill and suspense of being in turn hunter and hunted, is about discovery and being discovered.

One of the activities children most often refer to when describing their grandparents is playing. Grandparents are great playmates. Maybe their lives have turned back to a point where the fun and importance of play is self-evident. Grandparents are hard to embarrass, having become far less worried about what people think of them. I have seen many a grandparent covered in paint, crawling around the floor on all fours, tucking into mud pies and dressed in outrageous clothes. A grandfather of sixty stands outside a door in a cold corridor for being a naughty boy and cannot return to the warmth of the sitting-room until the four-year-old teacher calls him in to say sorry and to promise to be good. A grandmother lies on the ground outside in the garden, panting and barking and wanting to be let in for a pat and some dog biscuits. There is nothing patronising or sacrificial about the involvement of grandparents. Look at them closely and they will be as absorbed in the game as their grandchildren. It is this harmony that makes play so fulfilling and creates the very special closeness and unity that can exist between grandparent and grandchildren.

 Top Tip: *Grandparents know the importance of play and so make great playmates.*

Play can also be a means by which children come to terms with difficult life experiences and cope with their fears and anxieties. The trolls that are deadly in the dark can be turned to stone in the light. This type of play, which might explore the dark corners in a child's mind, will need to be with someone deeply trusted. The greater the range of trusted adults the better. Children can then choose to whom they go.

All Part of the Learning Experience

Human beings, compared with other animals, have a long period of immaturity. The time of dependency involves a long-term need for care and protection. This is normally provided by parents and others who share a measure of the caring role – and grandparents fit the role exactly. The advantage of this prolonged period is that it gives human beings a long time to absorb the knowledge and experience of their elders and to give weight to what is told to them by parents, teachers and grandparents. Effective communication underpins all this experience.

Top Tip: *Grandparents need to be good communicators.*

Play for younger children, more formal teaching and training for older children, are routes to intelligence and understanding. Rich and varied experiences in childhood build up a wide selection in the library of knowledge for a young person to draw upon. Grandparents, through their commitment and life experience, can provide some of the most precious volumes of all for this library.

The goal for our grandchildren is that, on becoming adults, they will be independent and self-directed – guided faithfully though life by their own inner wisdom.

Top Tip: *Wise grandparents can help their grand-children discover their own inner wisdom.*

Grandparents and School-Age Grandchildren

The Widening World

Starting School

It was late summer in the early 1970s. My wife and I with our son, our eldest child, found ourselves walking more and more slowly until we became like Shakespeare's schoolboy 'creeping like snail, unwillingly to school'. We were taking our son to his first day at school. The twist in our story was that it was Sally and I who were walking ever more slowly. In the end our son had to hurry us along. He did not want to be late for his first day. At the school, after a quick kiss and a wave, he strode

95

straight into the playground. Sally and I hung about outside the school gates, after he had vanished from sight, feeling like criminals who had abandoned their child. It might be his first day but, in a way, it was ours as well. It was a new experience for all three of us. Sally and I drooped around all day wondering what was happening in the alien world that had taken over our son. We were half expecting the phone to ring with a summons for us to collect him immediately. When we picked him up from school he skipped cheerfully home, provided a few, bare details about the day, wolfed down a huge tea and went off to play with his friends. Sally and I gathered our ordeal was over.

We remembered this first day when our young granddaughter started at her nursery school. There were many things from our own experience that we were able to share with our daughter and granddaughter before the big day arrived. There are many critical points in the lives of children. Starting school is one of the most important. It is at these times that the extra support and help of a grandparent can be welcome, not only for the grandchildren but for the parents as well. It is no good telling an anxious parent that starting school is something millions and millions of young people have achieved without the sky falling down. It will remain a unique occasion for the child and the parents. Grandparents are poised between the ordinary and the unique. They know that starting school is a normal enough part of any child's development but they will also understand the special quality of that moment for those particular parents and children.

Top Tip: *A child starting school is a stressful time for any parent and a key stage for grandparents to provide extra support.*

The Wide Wide World

Starting school is part of a child's entrance into life. The world suddenly becomes larger. Some former freedoms have to be sacrificed for the discipline of regular attendance and formal learning. One of the dangers for children at this time is that they will misjudge their abilities. They may feel too superior and thus open up the way to a heavy fall in the future. More likely, they may start to develop a sense of inadequacy and inferiority. They might doubt that they have the capacity to learn and develop new skills.

To avoid this, it is important to get the balance right between pressurised high expectations and indifferent low expectations. This is impossible unless you know the child well and understand what the child is capable of achieving. Expectations that are right for one child might be too high, or too low, for another. It all depends on their ability. Children who labour under unrealistically high expectations will live constantly with failure and this may eventually destroy their self-esteem. When the expectations of children are too low they will not be challenged and will find it hard to achieve their potential. Parents with too low expectations of their children are neglectful; those with too high expectations are stressful. A good parent will trust their instincts. They know their child and their child's capabilities better than anybody else. I have seen children suffering in both ways: children whose potential has been wasted and left to wither and to die; and children who have cracked under the selfishly high demands of parents. It is the potential of children that should be fulfilled; not the ambitions of parents.

Top Tip: Help your child get the balance right between having too high – or too low – expectations of their children.

If, as a society, we become addicted to tests, targets and league tables, the greatest danger will be to try to push children too far, too fast. I often hear parents trying to persuade us that their children should be in the category for the 'specially gifted'; I do not hear nearly so often parents talking openly about children who have special needs or who have difficulties coping at school. A success-driven society is not sympathetic to these children. But a grandparent is not driven by the success of the grandchild but by love. For grandparents there are no children in the world to be compared with their grandchildren, however successful the other children might be. The grandparent-as-fan can be uplifting for a struggling child. For a struggling parent too! My wife, who was a teacher, remembers grandparents coming to open evenings to support their children who were the parents of children having difficulties at school. How welcome they were.

> **Top Tip:** A grandparent's love for their grandchild should be defined by the fact that they are their grandchildren, rather than by the child's 'success'.

Grandparents are further from today's competitive edge and are less likely to push their grandchildren over it. Grandparents can also be very shrewd judges of the abilities of their grandchildren. I believe one of the most important pieces of advice that can be given to a loving parent or grandparent is for them to trust their judgement. No one knows their child/grandchild as well as they do.

Grandparents have the authority, and the position, to work with parents to help get the best out of their children. They can have a quiet and kind word with a parent suggesting they ease up if they are burdening a child with unrealistic expectations. On the other hand they can push for a greater interest in a child's development and suggest higher expectations should be set. Often grandparents are portrayed as loving push-overs but I have also known them to be formidable warriors if their grandchildren were not being treated with the respect their particular abilities deserved.

> **Top Tip:** Fight your grandchild's corner if you suspect that they aren't being treated with the respect that they, or their abilities, deserve.

If At First You Don't Succeed . . .

The world is a competitive place. Failure is inevitable. We all fail many times and, however good we are at something, there will be somebody better somewhere. Our grandchildren will fail, and will fail often, but they need to know we love them whether they win or lose. It is impossible to shield children from competition even if we wanted to. At the moment my young granddaughter will play only no-winning games. She cannot bear the idea that someone will be a loser, especially if that someone might be her! But eventually you cannot avoid games involving winning and losing, and healthy competition is a way for young people to test themselves out and to discover their own particular gifts and skills.

 Top Tip: *Grandchildren need to know we love them whether they win or lose.*

If children do well, they deserve recognition. They may deserve a pat on the back simply for having the courage to have a go. Children, like the rest of us, want to feel valued and appreciated so we should applaud them when we can. Grandparents make a great audience. However, it is important to avoid vague or unmeant, or even routine, praise as this gives children faulty feedback. Anyway children will suss out insincerity or carelessness quickly enough. But specific, genuine praise for a task done to the best of our ability can give us the encouragement to carry on striving and trying. Busy parents may miss an opportunity to praise their child so grandparents can provide valuable back-up, especially as grandparents have a priceless ability to make their grandchildren feel good about themselves.

 Top Tip: *Grandparents who are generous with their applause will help their grandchildren feel good about themselves.*

Life for any of us will never be a continuous run of praise-worthy accomplishments. We all make a hash of things. Grandparents can help their grandchildren cope with the custard pies that life keeps throwing in their faces. Though it does not feel like it at the time, failures can be the most valuable experiences any of us have. They provide vivid lessons if only we have the boldness to face them squarely and honestly. The gift a grandparent can offer is to make it clear to a grandchild that failure in a task does not make them a failure as a person. If grandchildren know they are operating from a base where they are loved, respected and admired they will have the security to venture further and further into the unknown future, learning from their failures and mistakes as they go. Grandparents themselves will many, many times have had to take the advice of the song to 'pick yourself up, dust yourself down and start all over again', and are consequently able to pass on this admirable philosophy to their grandchildren.

Top Tip: *The life experience of a grandparent means they are in a great position to encourage their grandchildren to persevere through hard times.*

Picking Up Signs

School is also where social life takes off. At school a great range of relationships opens up. These early relationships outside the family are going to be significant for the way a child develops a capacity to form relationships in the future. If they go wrong

they can cause the most excruciating emotional pain. Being rejected, neglected, bullied or scorned can cause lasting damage to a child. That is why it is just as important to spot if things are not right with the informal, social side of school as it is if things are not right with the formal, academic side.

School-age children may find it hard to talk about things that are going wrong. Problems in relationships are particularly likely to cause embarrassment. It is the shameful parts of ourselves that are the hardest to disclose. Sometimes it might be easier for children to confide in a grandparent rather than a mum or a dad. Grandparents represent safety; they are usually a little distance from the day-to-day intimacy that can make it so difficult to start a conversation that might prove painful.

Top Tip: *Your grandchild may find it easier to confide in you than their mum or dad.*

The Importance of Good Listening

Grandparents should try to make their grandchildren understand that there is nothing in the whole wide world too difficult to talk over with them. Once this confidence and trust is established grandparents will need to be good listeners and shrewd readers of the signs.

Grandparents are great at keeping secrets. I am the only person in the whole world who knows that the shelter on the platform of the little station where I live is not a shelter for waiting passengers. It does not belong to Railtrack. It is a magic house. Invisible people live there. It is the place belonging to my granddaughter, where she houses all kinds of characters from her imagination.

This role of being a special confidant is an important one for us as grandparents. If our grandchildren trust us, they may tell us things that are only to be between the two of us.

However, we must be careful never to promise our grandchildren too much. We should not promise to keep a secret, or respect a confidence, in all circumstances. There is an overriding responsibility to serve the best interests of our grandchildren. If we learn something from our grandchild that threatens their wellbeing we must take action, even if this means breaching a confidence (although we should never do this without explaining why to our grandchild).

 Top Tip: *Grandparents are good at keeping secrets, but should never promise to keep a secret at the cost of their grandchild's wellbeing.*

In the last chapter we considered the importance of communication. Listening is what makes effective communication possible. Most of us think we are good listeners but few of us are. It is an art that requires us to forget ourselves and to lose ourselves in another person. We need to be completely identified with that new person and every ounce of our concentration needs to be focused on what they are saying and the way they look and behave. Done well, listening is exhausting.

> **Top Tip:** *Listening is a complex skill and one in which we need to use all our other senses as well as our ears.*

Listening is also a way to show another person how much we value them. When we listen carefully we are silently communicating the words, 'You are worth listening to'. From the child's point of view if they see that they are heard (to mix two senses) they will draw the conclusions, 'I am worth being listened to'; 'They are interested in me'; 'They are taking what I say seriously'. Often what children say is not taken seriously so attentive listening is a big step towards building trust.

Good listening needs to be patient and persistent. If a subject is a stressful one children will rarely spell out everything in one go. They will approach it tentatively and may not reveal what

is bothering them until they have taken time to establish that you are the right person to confide in. Trust needs to be won. It does not drop on us without having been earned. None of us will invest in a relationship and commit ourselves to it without testing out first that it is reliable and durable. We should expect children to do the same.

 Top Tip: *Children will only confide in someone if they feel that they are truly being listened to.*

Grandchildren need to be able to read the signs. How often when we are feeling pretty awful do we respond to the question 'How are you?' with the answer 'All right'? Children are the same. Sometimes 'All right' can be no more than a way of putting off a more lengthy and truthful answer. A good friend sees beyond the words but, at the same time, does not try to force a confidence.

You might possibly succeed once in forcing somebody to say something when they are not ready but that person will not give you a chance to do it again. Open-ended questions to grandchildren like 'Do you want to tell me what's wrong?' or 'Do you remember you mentioned about something going wrong at school? Do you want to tell me anything more?' are ways of showing you have noticed something is up and that you care about it, while leaving your grandchild in charge of whether he says anything.

Actions Sometimes Speak Louder than Words

Watching out for non-verbal behaviour can help someone to see deeper than the words on the surface. For example, if you ask a grandchild if they had a good day at school and they reply 'yes' but, at the same time, without knowing it, shake their head, you might deduce that there is an unspoken message in the conflict between word and gesture. Similarly a child might look anxious, distracted or restless while saying that everything is fine. There is a volume of hidden words to be read in a single expression of unmistakable sadness in a child's eyes.

> **Top Tip:** As you listen, watch out for unspoken messages by paying attention to your grandchild's body language.

Creative listening, or active listening, are fancy terms for encouraging communication. It can be achieved by feeding back to a grandchild our understanding of how they might be feeling. For example, if grandchildren say they do not want to go to school it would be all too easy for a grandparent to say something like; 'Don't be silly, all the other children go', or 'Of course you want to go, schooldays are the happiest days of your life', or 'It'll be all right, don't you worry' (even though it is obvious that worried is exactly what the child is). These kinds of responses have two effects: they close down the

107

conversation and they deny the child's feelings. A better response is to say 'It sounds like you are a bit scared' or 'It sounds like something is happening at school you don't like'. We might not get it right but at least we are making it clear we have heard an underlying message. If we offer our view of the child's feelings we are both paying them respect and also leaving it open for the child to correct and improve our understanding. Even an open-ended question like 'Why don't you want to go to school?' keeps the conversation alive.

Top Tip: *The more open-ended your questions, the more likely you are to get a response.*

But we must beware. Responding sensitively takes time and trouble and we cannot rely on these opportunities to come at a good moment. Children may announce they do not want to go to school when we are running late and desperately trying to get everything ready for the day. If we sense a child is expressing something very important these opportunities should not be missed. Daily demands are always with us. The chance to confront a problem before it becomes too serious might not come again. These conversations are important because they make it possible to identify and overcome potentially damaging experiences in a child's life. If something is going wrong at school it is important to discover the nature of the problem. It might be a difficulty with a particular subject or a particular teacher. It might be the first inkling that a child suffers from a condition that makes learning difficult. It might be that the child is being bullied. Whatever it is it can only be tackled if it is known.

 Top Tip: *Whenever a child wants to talk seriously about something, however inconvenient it is, always take the opportunity.*

It is hard to welcome problems and the suffering that often accompanies them. Grandparents, with their own experience behind them, will know that life has much of its meaning in meeting and solving problems. Problems call forth our courage and wisdom. Grandparents can teach their grandchildren the value of facing up bravely to the hard knocks of life. It is tackling the tough things that helps us to grow stronger.

Bullying

The courage to square up to a problem is particularly important in the case of bullying. Many schools have made progress in tackling bullying through a variety of innovative measures. However, when I was working for the NSPCC time and again I heard it claimed 'Bullying does not happen at this school' when the evidence made clear that it most certainly did. Bullying is far more prevalent, and its consequences far more serious, than our society accepts. This denial by the adult world fails the bully, whose behaviour is left unchecked, and the bullied, who is left unprotected. Bullying needs to be addressed as an unacceptable feature of our society. Bullies have to be confronted. Usually the victim is not strong enough to do this without help.

 Top Tip: *Grandparents can work alongside parents in helping children regain their confidence and stand up to bullies.*

It is often not easy to admit to being bullied. It might well be a grandparent in whom a child first confides. From that moment it should be a problem faced and a problem shared. Grandparents are part of the front-line forces that can be called up to help defend a vulnerable child. The response should not be one of aggressive retaliation as this simply confirms the way of the bully. Nor should any intervention undermine the bullied child's self-confidence. The approach must be one that reinforces the worth of the bullied child and builds up their own strength. This is not easy to achieve but all who are involved need to be undaunted; otherwise we only confirm the victim's worst fear that bullying cannot be resisted. A well-supported and loved child who is dealing with the problem with caring adults and friends is far more likely to overcome the bully than the child left in isolation to suffer a lonely humiliation in the dark corner of a playground.

The Stress Epidemic

Even without the experience of bullying the world can be a stressful place for children. There is so much to worry about, whether it be about failing exams, being ugly, having no friends or simply about being different. Stress has reached epidemic proportions in the Western world and children are not safe from it. A survey by the Mental Health Association suggested that up to a fifth of all children suffered from a disorder related to stress. One of the beauties of the grandparent–grandchild relationship is that it can be a stress-free zone. Grandparents and grandchildren are not rivals or competitors and have nothing to prove to each other. They are free to enjoy each other's company for its own sake. This freedom from external pressure can help make the relationship a healing one, for grandparents and grandchildren alike. The homes of grandparents can become safe havens offering rest cures directly to stressed-out grandchildren (and indirectly to stressed-out parents!).

 Top Tip: *Try to make your home seem like a stress-free zone for your grandchildren.*

A Healing Hand

Problems occur not only outside but also can happen within the family. All parents and children fall out and go through bad patches. At such times grandparents – standing outside the intense relationship of parent and child, but inside the family – should be prepared to be mediators and conciliators. Concerned for both parties, grandparents are ideally placed to help rebuild the broken bridges between grandchildren and their parents.

MUM AND GRANDMA AREN'T SPEAKING OVER THE FACT THAT I KEEP SHOUTING..

As experienced witnesses of family life, grandparents can spot problems other members of the family are too close to notice. Using keen observation and the instincts that come from experience grandparents can be great healers too, able to touch those hurt bits that other cures can't reach.

Top Tip: *Grandparents can be key in helping to rebuild broken bridges.*

Discipline

I do not want to finish this chapter without commenting on that fraught subject – discipline. The controversy in the UK surrounding the discipline of children is not so much about discipline itself but about the way to deliver it. All of us involved with children should agree they need discipline. Total freedom from limits is impossible in this life. Discipline is not about giving up freedom; it is about growing a self-confident, personal freedom to lead a full life in a world full of other people with freedoms too. It is only through discipline that children can learn about boundaries, about right and wrong and about respecting other people. Discipline provides the framework for our values. Indeed I believe that for children to be denied loving and consistent discipline is a form of child abuse in itself.

 Top Tip: *Loving, consistent discipline provides a secure framework within which a child can grow and develop.*

However, it is important to stress in this discussion about discipline that unless grandparents are custodians, or have full-time care of their grandchildren, their role is supplementary. The discipline of children is the responsibility of their parents. The buck stops with the parents. To blame the bad behaviour or the lack of self-discipline of their children on others, or the world at large, is to try to escape a responsibility belonging to parents. For example, I am amazed by the expectations some parents have of schools. These parents seem to believe it is the job of teachers to teach their children the difference between right and wrong and how to behave.

 Top Tip: *Discipline is the primary responsibility of a parent, but grandparents can play a crucial supporting role.*

Although no parent should try to duck out of their ultimate responsibility for disciplining their children, or to try to shove it onto someone else, most parents will appreciate a helping hand in exercising their authority. Thus it is appropriate to see providing discipline as a partnership between parents and other caring figures in a child's life, such as teachers and close relatives.

Some parents have a very hard time of it, for any number of reasons, and to offer condemnation rather than support is not only unkind but it is also counterproductive. The vast majority of parents want to do the best for their children; it is just that some of us need more help than others. Who better to help than a grandparent?

A detailed examination of the ways to provide discipline belongs more to a discussion about parenting but I want to conclude this chapter with a few points of particular relevance for grandparents:

1 Discipline Should Be Consistent
Children need consistency. They will be confused by mixed, contradictory and arbitrary messages. They cannot develop robust self-discipline without a firm and reliable foundation. It is essential that grandparents work with parents to make sure that together they provide this consistency. The subject of discipline should be openly discussed.

Top Tip: *Discipline must be consistent. Grandchildren will only be confused if they receive one message from their parents and another from you.*

Any differences of opinion should be ironed out by the adults and not taken out on the child. In the final count, unless something is seriously wrong, if consensus cannot be reached it is the parents' disciplining line that should always be followed. Remember, though, that consistency is not the same as uniformity. Grandparents are revered by their grandchildren as the kind of people with whom you can get away with things that are not possible anywhere else. Long may grandparents remain as these loving 'soft touches', but this should not be carried to the point where it leads to fundamental inconsistencies and to confused and manipulated grandchildren.

An example of an inconsistent approach is the case of friends of mine who were trying to teach their overweight children about looking after their teeth, a good diet and self-discipline about sweets, only to discover that their children were allowed unlimited access to a hugely stocked drawer of sweets and chocolates on their frequent visits to their grandparents' house, and were always excused the irksome task of cleaning their teeth whenever they stayed the night.

By contrast, another friend was struggling to cope with the behaviour of her fourteen-year-old stepdaughter. My friend, the stepmother, had not been accepted by the daughter after her father had married again following the death of his first wife. The stepmother was a committed Christian and the fourteen-year-old consistently challenged her values. The crunch came when the stepdaughter started going out with an older man and was open about having unprotected sex with him. The daughter was confined to home in the evenings and not allowed to see her boyfriend on her own. She and the boyfriend went to the police and claimed she was being abused and falsely imprisoned. As a compromise the daughter agreed to have a 'cooling-off period' living with her grandparents. These were the parents of her dead mother. They were not Christians and had had difficulty themselves accepting the second wife. They had been indulgent in their relationship with their granddaughter who had always been spoilt by them. The granddaughter was confident of a sympathetic hearing. Imagine, then, her surprise when she started complaining bitterly about her stepmother, only to be told by her grandparents that they completely agreed with the stepmother and fully backed and supported everything she had done. Not all the problems stopped overnight but, when the stepdaughter returned, she was a chastened character and had started to realise her stepmother was not picking on her but acting on a loving concern.

 Top Tip: *When fair discipline is challenged, grandparents should stand shoulder to shoulder with the parents.*

---

2 Discipline Should Be Well Prepared

Discipline should not be impulsive and arbitrary but thought-through and backed up by a recognisable moral code. All children, however well behaved, are likely to test out the boundaries of discipline. This can be particularly true of grandchildren. They might want to check for any disharmony in the relationship between their parents and grandparents.

Top Tip: *Children may play on any disharmony they sense in the relationship between their parents and grandparents.*

In these cases it helps to prepare in advance. I remember how, when we were caring for our older grandchildren for half-term, a fierce challenge was mounted by our eleven-year-old grandson concerning what videos he should be allowed to watch. A firm assurance was given that his parents regularly allowed him to watch videos with a '15' classification. Indeed it was implied that if we were the kind of grandparents who really wanted their grandchildren to have a good time (as, of course, we were) then it would only be natural for us to allow him to watch full-blooded and full-frontal adult videos. 'All my friends watch them', he said, which might well have been true. The assault was rendered a little less plausible when our nine-year-old granddaughter piped up with the assurance that her parents allowed her to watch everything her brother did. Fortunately Sally and I had discussed this beforehand with our son and daughter-in-law so we knew that they enforced strict control over the videos the children were allowed to watch. Videos with a '15' classification were not allowed.

There was a short period of discontent that half-term during which Sally and I were made to feel like proper spoilsports. However, it did not last and it was more than made up for by the fact that the testing out was soon abandoned when it became clear that, on all important matters, the house rules with us were the same as at home.

 Top Tip: *On important issues, your house rules for your grandchildren should be the same as at their home.*

The Exception to the Rule

Sometimes, of course, parents are unreasonable or uncaring in the discipline they provide. This could apply if the parents are providing little discipline or guidance. In these situations, the grandparent must act. The task for the grandparent might then be to try and persuade the parents to take greater responsibility for the children. It is always best for parents to lead in matters of discipline but, as a last resort, grandparents should try to make good what is lacking and provide a disciplinary framework of their own to compensate for the parents' emotional neglect. Many people have testified to the moral lessons they have learnt through their relationships with grandparents.

The exception can also apply in the opposite circumstance

of parents who provide harsh or brutal discipline. Discipline is too often considered to require punitive penalties involving the infliction of pain or enforced coercion. At the NSPCC I saw many families where children were frequently and severely punished in the name of discipline. Their children were constantly shouted at, slapped, strapped, punched or beaten. They did not grow up to be law-abiding citizens. Too often they grew up to carry violence and abuse into the next generation.

Faced with this level of ill-treatment a loving grandparent has no choice but to confront it. The violence needs to be condemned. Attempts have to be made to persuade the parents to adopt more moderate, positive and effective forms of discipline. Sometimes parents are unreasonably harsh because they are afraid they do not have the capacity to be good parents. If they could be helped to have more confidence in themselves they might not need to cover their own anxieties in a show of aggression.

 Top Tip: If you think your grandchild is being ill-treated, you must confront the issue.

With children suffering from brutal approaches to discipline, grandparents will want to provide a haven where the impact of such treatment is softened. They will want to reassure their grandchildren that they are loved and that the excessive discipline they are experiencing is because of something wrong in their parents rather than something wrong in them. Once children become convinced they are bad there is nothing to stop them being bad.

 Top Tip: *Grandchildren, despite what may be going on around them, will be reassured by grandparents who love and believe in them.*

---

3 Discipline Needs to Be Disciplined and to Have Meaning

Discipline should always be for the good of the child and not for the relief or gratification of the adult. It should not be arbitrary or unpredictable. The meaning of an act of discipline should always be explained and made clear to a child, otherwise it is pointless.

4 Discipline Requires Time and Requires Us to Lead by Example

Effective discipline demands that we know children well as individuals, that we understand their particular strengths and weaknesses and that we know what kinds of discipline works with them. Time and patience is needed to explain why discipline is necessary and to examine and consider moral issues together. Grandparents often have more time for this than parents.

Although it might make more demands on us than we like, we need to practise what our discipline preaches. Children quickly detect hypocrisy. Like adults they are more likely to make judgements based on deeds rather than words. The 'do-as-I-say-not-as-I-do' approach never works because children will see that we value our own advice and instruction so little that we are not prepared to follow it ourselves.

If children see their parents and grandparents behaving without love, self-discipline, restraint, dignity or a capacity to order their own lives, then children will come to believe, in the deepest part of their being, that this is the right way to live. If, however, children see their parents and grandparents behaving with love, self-discipline, restraint, dignity and a capacity to order their own lives, then children will come to believe instead, in the deepest part of their being, that this is really the right way to live.

Ultimately discipline is part of love and is lost without it.

Grandparents and Teenagers

The Trapeze Artists

In Jane Wagner's play, *The Search for Signs of Intelligent Life in the Universe*, there is a character with the striking name of Agnus Angst. Agnus is an adolescent who has fallen out with her parents in a big way. 'The last really deep conversation I had with Dad', she recalls, 'was between our T-shirts. His said "Science is Truth Found Out". Mine said, "The truth can be made up if you know how".'

Agnus is thrown out by her parents and goes to live with her grandparents. It is not a happy arrangement as Agnus makes clear: 'I have other family, my grandparents, but we have nothing in common, except that we are all carbon-based life forms.' The grandparents, Lud and Marie, are appalled by their granddaughter's behaviour and appearance. They complain that their 'pink-haired granddaughter's got the manners of a terrorist' and, what is more, she 'wears something [that] makes the garage door flap up'.

Few relationships between parents and adolescents break down as completely as did Agnus' relationship with her parents. Nevertheless, the teenage years are often a particularly stressful period for both parents and children. Grandparents can be a great source of strength at these times as long as they are more in touch with their grandchildren than Lud and Marie were with Agnus.

A Turbulent Time

The adolescent years have often been described as an age of transition. Adolescence is a stage between childhood and adulthood. This vision of in-betweenness can be useful in explaining how the adolescent can seem like an immature child one minute and a mature adult the next. It can help too in emphasising the turbulent changes a teenager is experiencing in mind, body and spirit as they move through the final stages of childhood's growth to independence. Many a parent has been stunned by a cheerful, cuddly child, who loved to be kissed goodnight and read a bedtime story, suddenly turning into a moody teenager with a stud in the nose, a ring through the lip and a tattoo on the bottom spelling out 'Hands off'. However, recognition of the strain parents can suffer should never make us lose sight of how hard a time adolescence can be for the teenagers themselves.

Another advantage of seeing adolescence as an in-between

age is that it draws attention to the fact that it does not last forever. Although this seems an obvious statement to make, the truth is that parents who are caught up in the day-to-day conflicts of living with teenage children can easily succumb to the fear that there is no way out. Grandparents, having had children of their own who were teenagers and are now parents, are able to offer encouraging and timely reminders that this stage, as every other, does eventually end. Having the end in mind, apart from keeping a light burning at the end of the tunnel, can also help parents to manage the transition in such a way as to ensure their relationship with their children is intact when adolescence is over.

 Top Tip: *Grandparents can reassure their children that their own teenager's traumas will not last forever!*

What Really Matters

To serve the purpose of preserving a loving relationship with their children, parents need judgement in deciding what is worth making an issue of and what is best left alone. During adolescence it is almost certain clashes will occur over subjects such as dress, appearance, behaviour, school work, friends, interests, habits and social activities. If parents and their teenagers are at loggerheads with each other all the time, over just about everything, then the parents are in danger of losing authority and influence when these are still very much needed. With respect for the age and development of their children, and allowing for adolescence being a time for experimentation and increasing independence, parents need to decide which battles should be fought and which can, and should, be avoided. Grandparents can reinforce and influence their children's judgements. We can remember the advice and discipline that was helpful to us as teenagers and all the advice and orders we ignored; hopefully, we will also have learnt from the mistakes we made as parents and will be keen to prevent these being repeated in the next generation.

 Top Tip: Grandparents can help their children to decide which battles are worth fighting with their teenager.

It is said that as you get older your long-term memory improves as your short-term memory deteriorates. Grandparents are likely to be able to remember not one but two generations of adolescence; our own and our children's. With the passing of time, these distant memories are less locked in time and can be recovered to use as yardsticks by which to gauge adolescent development.

I have already made a passing reference to my own adolescence. With my friend I was, for a period, part of a group of rebellious and badly behaved ne'er-do-wells. However, because we were lucky enough not to get into serious trouble, most of us ended up doing well enough. I can judge my behaviour then by the much higher standards I have now, while at the same time remembering that I should not be the first to cast a stone at today's teenager.

> **Top Tip:** *Look back in time. The social context may have changed, but you'll see that your teenage grandchild probably isn't very different from how you and your children were as teenagers.*

Then being a parent of teenage children brought new lessons and fresh experiences. Sally and I had three children but only one adolescent! Our first two children worried us as teenagers because they were so conscientious, decent and hardworking. We found ourselves offering such worldly advice as 'Why don't you forget your homework for once and go out and enjoy yourself?' Our relationship with our youngest daughter proved a far more typical struggle, with Sally and me constantly saying things like 'You must stay in and do some homework; otherwise you'll never pass your exams and then what will you do?' or 'If you are going out tonight we don't want you coming back after midnight, legless and with your drunken friends'. With my youngest daughter, as words were abandoned as a means of communication, I became a world expert at interpreting grunts. I could soon easily distinguish between the grunt which meant: 'Well if I have to say "good morning" to you this is as close as I will get'; and the grunt which meant: 'You are so embarrassing I wish you would vanish from my life forever.' I came to doubt if we would ever have a proper conversation again. But we did. My youngest daughter has become a successful and hardworking dentist and we now occasionally share memories from her adolescence and have a good laugh together. However turbulent these years might be, by hanging in there it is possible for teenagers who have grown up to look back on them with their parents in a shared humorous detachment.

 Top Tip: When your child is feeling overwhelmed by their own teenager, gently remind them what they were like when they were younger (and that they – and you – survived!).

It is this kind of perspective that grandparents can bring when they have teenage grandchildren. Grandparents are the embodiment of hope. They are witnesses to the fact that time passes and that rebellious teenagers can become responsible adults. Grandparents can help with the judgements about what is important and what is only to be expected.

 Top Tip: *Grandparents can bring new optimism to their children with the knowledge that even the most rebellious teenager can turn into a responsible adult.*

As Old as the Hills

Of course, sometimes, adolescence can be a time when life goes seriously wrong for a young person and then they will need all the persevering care, guidance and support a family, including grandparents, can provide. However, in many cases, grandparents can simply reassure a beleaguered parent that much of what they are worrying about is normal. What parents consider to be uniquely awful about their children might be little more than par for the teenage course.

And there is nothing new about these problems. Although adolescence has been described as a modern invention and the conflicts between teenagers and parents seen as a special feature of contemporary society, they in fact go back hundreds of years. You may be familiar with the following quotation:

The world is going through troubled times. Today's young people only think of themselves. They've got no respect for parents or old people. They've got no time for rules and regulations. To hear them talk, you'd think they knew everything. And what we think of as wise, they just see as foolish. As for the girls, they don't speak, act or dress with any kind of modesty or feminine grace.

And that was written by Peter the Monk as long ago as AD 1274!

Moving from the dependence of the child to the independence of the adult is too significant a change to happen overnight. Young people have to grow into independence. They need time to experiment, to argue, to test out limits, to make their own decisions and, increasingly, to take responsibility for their lives. They need their parents, and grandparents, to guide them through this transition. It will require a lot of guidance in the early stages and less and less towards the end.

An Experienced Guide

Parents may find it difficult to pace themselves through this process. With the first signs of their children growing up, and growing away, some parents give up immediately. An either/or situation can develop. Either adolescents have to continue to accept everything their parents say or they can go and do what they like. This black-and-white approach is summed up in the words of the irate father who told his daughter, 'You can do what I say or you can go and get lost.' Which is what she did. She went and got lost.

Adolescence is a mountainous region. There are perilous ascents to be made and falls are inevitable. For children to go without an experienced guide and companion can be dangerous.

 Top Tip: Grandparents can help their children hang on as parents so that their teenagers are not left without a guide.

Decisions for parents with adolescent children are rarely black-and-white ones; they are in the grey zone. This is a time for

131

compromise, negotiation and discussion. Reasons have to be offered where once the parental word was sufficient. Authority ceases to be given and has to be earned. Mistakes and misunderstandings are likely on both sides of the relationship so it is a time for parents to take a lead – to have the courage to admit mistakes and say sorry.

Grandparents who are able to recognise the continuing needs of their grandchildren can provide the guidance and example that encourage parents to stay involved and to keep working at it. Underneath a cool exterior teenagers are often confused and insecure. Grandparents may be able to see under the surface. We know that teenagers continue to need encouragement and praise when it is earned. We know you are never, ever, too old to be told you are loved.

 Top Tip: *During the teenage years, grandparents can play a crucial role in loving both their children and their teenage grandchildren at a time when each might feel unloved.*

If the relationship between parents and their teenage children breaks down then grandparents may need to act. If teenagers are going astray, and losing their way, non-interference ceases to be an option. A good grandparent will get stuck in. The evidence of young people shows that many of them have been saved from drug addiction, prostitution and other serious problems by active grandparents who were prepared to get involved when the going got tough.

> **Top Tip:** If you think the relationship between parent and teenager is in danger of breaking down, get involved.

Learning to Let Go

Every loving parent finds it difficult to let go, but sometimes the problem is particularly apparent. They find it impossible first to delegate, and then relinquish, their authority over their child. They cannot bear the prospect of losing their dependent little child. In these cases, it's entirely understandable that adolescents feel that they have little option but to rebel and insist on their right to become independent. The alternative is that the young person never fully achieves maturity. The way parents maintain a smothering influence is usually by changing from an authoritative approach to one that makes the young person feel guilty about growing up. Possessiveness in parents is brutal in its consequences. It stunts growth, sours relationships, denies freedom and reaches its climax by destroying love. You have to be free to love. However painful it might be, a loving parent knows when to let go.

Grandparents know all about letting go. Hopefully they have done it themselves. They can help their children, when parents, to allow their grandchildren to grow up. It is part of a constant, recurring cycle of human growth.

133

Top Tip: *Grandparents can help parents come to terms with letting go, because they've done it themselves.*

Making the Most of Your Position

Studies of grandparents have shown they tend to have relationships with their grandchildren comparatively free from conflict. This is to be expected, especially with older children, because issues of authority and dependency are not so central to a grandparent–grandchild relationship. Children do not have to struggle to separate themselves from grandparents nor fight with them for independence. Also a new generation needs characteristics of its own if it is to be distinguished from the previous generation. But the generation before that is no threat – it is history. Grandparents are a safe distance from the family battleground of adolescence but close enough to be concerned about the sound of distant gunfire.

Top Tip: *Grandparents make great mediators. Your unique position means that you can help to resolve conflicts without getting caught in the crossfire.*

GRANDPA, TELL
DAD I'M NOT
SPEAKING TO HIM
TILL HE STOPS INSISTING
THAT I SPEAK TO
MY GRANDPARENTS
MORE
OFTEN!

The comparative tranquillity of the relationship with grand-parents gives them an influential position with their grand-children. Grandparents make good mediators and healers. If it comes to a crunch at home the relationship can be extended to provide sanctuary for a grandchild. This can provide relief and a time for cooling-off. However, it should always be a temporary arrangement that ends when parent and child are reunited.

The Big Issues

Another way grandparents can use their influence is in a willingness to talk about the big subjects. Studies have shown that older children may find it easier to talk to their grandparents than their parents. So grandparents can help parents to make sure that big issues do not get ducked, whether they be sex, drugs or rock and roll. Many people find it embarrassing to talk about these subjects but they should not be left for others outside the family to deal with. Children should have the opportunity of exploring these topics in a loving relationship with someone they trust. They should be helped to share their fears and encouraged to develop their own opinions. Nor should the first step be left to the children, who will be embarrassed too. It is up to adults to take the initiative. If an important subject does not crop up naturally in conversation grandparents should be bold enough to raise it themselves.

Top Tip: *Grandchildren will often find it easier to talk to their grandparents about the big issues.*

Take sex, for example. Even though we are surrounded and bombarded by sexual images, most of us find sex hard to talk about seriously. It might be an especially tough proposition for grandparents brought up in more reticent and reserved times. I remember the excitement of getting into an 'X' film, under age, when there was the tantalising possibility of catching a glimpse of something you can now see every day in some newspapers. If the 1960s were permissive how on earth do we describe the 1990s? (Perhaps the first decade of the twenty-first century really should be called the naughties!) Children today have to deal with far more open and explicit sexual material than did their grandparents. However, grandparents have one considerable advantage in talking about sex – our grandchildren will presume we gave it up years ago. Grandparents can help a young person to avoid seeing sex as a subject on its own and to see it instead within the context of values and relationships. Grandparents will be only too well aware that, if teenagers cannot talk about it, the only way to find out about it is to try it.

 Top Tip: *Grandparents can help their grandchildren see sex within the context of values and relationships.*

Similarly with drugs, grandparents are likely to be seen as safely distant from the contemporary drug scene. Grandchildren would be astonished to know that their grandparents once experimented with drugs in their youth although a good many of them will have done just that. The authority of grandparents comes from their experience of life. Based on their experience they can testify to the devastating effects on young lives the misuse of drugs can have. As well as being a threat to life, and to health, drugs can deprive a young person of any hope of reaching independence by simply swapping one, healthy form of dependency for another, lethal kind. It will help to maintain the relevance of what grandparents say if they can keep in touch with the ways problems develop.

 Top Tip: *Grandparents will be able to offer better informed help if they keep in touch with their teenage grandchildren and understand the problems they face.*

How Do I Look?

Grandparents are free to tell it the way they see it. They do not have to pull any punches. They can be unequivocal about their values. Given the immense pressures on teenagers from their peer group, their culture and their own generation, the more varied the knowledge, advice and beliefs they come into contact with the more they are truly free to make up their own minds. The views of grandparents, based on years of experience, can be a counterbalance to the view of the contemporary scene.

Young people are thinking deeply about a wide range of issues such as drugs, bullying, crime, the environment, war, famines and family break-ups. But, in addition to the big subjects, there are matters the world at large might consider relatively unimportant but which can, in extreme circumstances, lead to depression, even suicide.

For example, many young people are desperately worried about their appearance. A survey conducted in 1998 by the

Schools Health Education Unit found that for fourteen- and fifteen-year-olds, out of all the categories surveyed, their biggest worry was 'the way you look' (by a small margin for boys but by a huge one for girls).

For those living and working closely with teenagers, some of their concerns might seem self-centred and superficial. As grandparents, we can be among those who understand that sudden bursts of growth, and the changes to their bodies, make young people sensitive and anxious about what is happening to them. Pressure to do well in exams, to decide on careers, to choose (and be chosen as) friends and to leave home can add to the burdens teenagers feel loaded upon them. Grandparents can help by recognising and accepting the sensitivity that goes with adolescence and by assisting their grandchildren to reach the precious self-confidence that will enable them to carry the weight of being responsible for themselves.

Top Tip: *Grandparents can see beneath the surface and recognise that even a cool teenager needs help developing self-esteem.*

Taking an Active Interest

In trying to be of help the most frequently mentioned concern of grandparents is that the world in which they grew up is so different from the one in which their grandchildren are growing up. In one sense this is not a problem. Grandparents are special because they belong to a different generation and have a different history and different kinds of experience. They are ancestral storehouses of tales and memories from a different time. However, these differences can be a problem if they lead to failures in communication and an inability to share interests.

To deal with this problem we need to try to avoid misunderstandings and resist jumping to premature conclusions. One pious grandmother was outraged when her granddaughter returned from Sunday school and said, 'Jesus is wicked.' It would have avoided a painful clash if the grandmother had taken time to discover that being 'wicked' is now positively complimentary.

It helps if grandparents are able to take an interest in the world of their grandchildren. There is nothing so boring as being with somebody who shows total indifference to all your interests. Grandparents can never immerse themselves completely in the present generation but they can watch their grandchildren's favourite television programme, read their favourite book, learn how to use a computer and even try listening to their favourite music. These activities are self-defeating if done in a negative or patronising manner but, if done out of genuine interest, can lead to common ground for grandparents to occupy with their grandchildren.

Besides, in continuing to seek new interests and broaden their experience, grandparents can help to keep themselves out of a geriatric rut. I recently found myself taking my oldest grandson to see the film *Dude, Where's My Car?* at his request. Sitting ankle-deep in popcorn I was the only person in the audience over the age of twenty! I am afraid what little street cred I had won I proceeded to lose by laughing in all the wrong places and failing to laugh in the right ones. I cannot say the experience converted me to a love of adolescent American humour, but it did provide my grandson and me with many opportunities to share our views and to relive some of the funnier moments. Indeed they seemed funnier when my grandson retold them than they had in the film!

 Top Tip: *Although much of it may seem alien to you, try to keep abreast of what's going in within your grandchild's world.*

In addition to aiding understanding and communication, staying in touch with contemporary developments can also help grandparents in their roles as protectors and guardians. For example, being aware what the lyrics of a modern song actually say leaves grandparents free to try to combat any influences they might consider harmful. Even more relevant is to know what is available on the Internet and how it can be used. There are many examples of young people being groomed for relationships with highly unsuitable adults through the Internet. Groups such as paedophiles were among the first to recognise the potential of the Internet to serve their purpose. The Internet is a vast library of information and most of its functions are useful and beneficial but, like most technological advances, it can be used for the wrong reasons as well as the right ones.

I do not want to overstate the importance of grandparents staying in touch with the contemporary scene as many grandparents will be loved partly for the very fact that they are blissfully indifferent to the world as it is now, but the more in touch a grandparent is the more they can help their grandchildren deal with the pressures of modern life.

 Top Tip: By being 'switched on' you can help protect your grandchild from possibly harmful influences.

Circus Tricks

At the beginning of this chapter we considered adolescence as an in-between stage; a stage between being a child and being an adult. It is the stage when the move from dependence to independence is finally accomplished. Many images have been used to describe this process. Perhaps the most fanciful is to see the adolescent as a chrysalis preparing to change and break out as a beautiful butterfly. My favourite picture sees the young person as a trapeze artist who has boldly let go of one trapeze (childhood) and is flying, arms outstretched, to catch the other trapeze (adulthood). During this perilous journey through space grandparents, alongside parents, can help to form the safety net beneath the mid-air artist.

However, if this view of the in-between stage is taken too far it can be counter-productive. Seeing young people only as some form of intermediate life form can deprive them of any value in their own right. They become a blank, a space between the child and the adult, neither one thing nor the other, neither fish nor fowl. Young people are people. Every teenager is a unique person with needs of their own. We should aim to nurture the individuality of our adolescent grandchild and to proclaim that a sixteen-year-old is as much a vital, needy, loveable and special human being as a six-year-old or a 66-year-old.

Top Tip: As everything around them changes, you can be crucial in reassuring your teenage grandchild that they are loved and valued as an individual in their own right.

Grandparents in the Front Line

Righting the Most Profound Wrong

Looking into the Shadows

I come now to the most difficult chapter to write, but I couldn't be true to my experience of children and families if I didn't tackle the issue of child abuse. It is easy to pretend that child abuse does not happen or, if it does, it only happens elsewhere, to other people's children, or to other people's grandchildren. In our hearts we know this is not the case. And it isn't. Child abuse can occur anywhere. It shows no respect for boundaries whether they be drawn by class, wealth, age or geography. At the NSPCC when child abuse was discovered we would often be greeted with sentiments like: 'I never believed it could happen here'; 'You hear of it happening but I never believed it could

145

happen in my family'; 'He seemed such a nice man. You couldn't believe he would be capable of harming a child.' There is something incomprehensible for many of us about child abuse. Even after working with children and families for over thirty years, fifteen of them at the NSPCC, I still find it hard to believe what some people are prepared to do to children. But it happens. It has to be believed. It must never be dismissed or simply accepted as a way of life. Child abuse has to be tackled. In the United Kingdom, between one and two children die every week following child abuse and neglect. Hundreds more suffer as a result of unspeakable acts of cruelty. These children are all likely to have grandparents.

Top Tip: *Grandparents are as important as anyone in the fight against child abuse.*

At the outset I must stress that it is important to strike a balance when considering child abuse. We must maintain a sense of proportion. Too often the debate swings from one extreme to the other. At one extreme huge numbers of children are claimed to have been abused with the whole young population immediately at risk; at the other extreme it is claimed that the numbers involved are negligible and that the whole subject has been vastly exaggerated. As usual the truth lies between the extremes. We should not be imposing restricted lives on our children for fear there is an abuser lurking round every corner. (Nor, in my opinion, should we be denying children hugs, or other signs of genuine affection, for fear of how they might be interpreted.

146

What a cold world we will create if touching becomes outlawed.) But we should never ignore the dangers of child abuse, deny its seriousness, nor fail to take sensible measures to protect our children. Much of this responsibility belongs to parents but grandparents will be involved as well. Not infrequently the intervention of grandparents into the lives of vulnerable children has led to them getting the help they needed.

 Top Tip: *In tackling child abuse, we must maintain a sense of proportion and use our judgement, but never hesitate to act if we suspect it.*

In Argentina a group of brave and determined grandmothers formed a group known as *Las Abuelas De Plaza De May* (Grandmothers of May Square). They were outraged by the plight of children who had been kidnapped after armed forces seized control of Argentina's government in 1976. These grandmothers, supported by lawyers and doctors, successfully located some of the lost children, most of whom have now been returned to their families. Given that many of the parents had been taken away and killed, the people to whom the children were returned were often their grandparents. So grandparents can act to protect their grandchildren even in the most difficult circumstances.

147

Top Tip: *Grandparents have been among the people at the forefront of protecting children from abuse.*

Thinking the Unthinkable

Grandparents need to be alert for signs of all kinds of abuse, physical, emotional, and sexual abuse as well as neglect. However, although it must be remembered that physical cruelty remains the most common form of abuse, the points made in the rest of this chapter are most relevant to suspected cases of sexual abuse.

Top Tip: *Don't look for demons under every bed, but always be alert for all the signs of child abuse.*

What Is Child Sexual Abuse?

It's a fair question and various definitions have been used. In its pamphlet 'Stopping Sexual Abuse Within the Family', the NSPCC states: 'Child sexual abuse is the term used when an adult uses a child for his or her own sexual pleasure and gratification. Both boys and girls can be abused from a very early age.'

In order to show just how far this is from having a cuddle or hug, the NSPCC gives examples of what the sexual abuse of children might include

- vaginal or anal intercourse;
- oral/genital contact or sex;
- masturbation between adults and children;
- encouraging or forcing children to prostitute themselves;
- use of children in pornographic filming or photographs.

Such a list makes painful reading but it helps us to get a glimpse of what children have to endure when they are sexually abused.

 Top Tip: However tough we might find the subject of child abuse, think what it is like for the child who is a victim.

Practical Steps

So what should grandparents do if they suspect cruelty to their grandchildren? How should they respond if they hear heart-stopping words, such as: 'Gran, Daddy does something to me I don't like'? The first need of the grandparent might be to overcome their own reactions. Some have felt faint and physically sick when it has dawned on them what might be happening to their grandchildren. One grandparent described it as 'like having a terrible nightmare only to discover that you are not asleep but wide awake'.

WHAT'S THE WISEST THING YOUR GRANDPARENTS EVER SAID TO YOU?

THAT THEY'RE ALWAYS READY TO SHUT UP AND LISTEN TO ME.

The one fact that might help a grandparent to take courage and manage their shock is that their grandchild needs them desperately and has chosen to put their trust in them. A child who has suffered abuse is very likely to find it agonising to talk about. Sometimes children are threatened with terrible things if they tell anybody. Consequently they will go only to a person they trust in a big way. This might well mean you. Grandparents 'fit' because they are well-loved figures who are not as close to the abuse as other members of the family, such as the non-offending parent.

Top Tip: *Abused children often choose to confide in their grandparents first.*

A grandchild in these circumstances will need to be comforted and made to feel safe. Then the grandparent should listen and keep on listening. We considered the importance of listening in an earlier chapter, and attentive listening now becomes more important than ever. Some of what children have to say might take all their courage to say and so it will help them if they do not have to repeat themselves. They will also need to know that they have been heard and understood. It will help to ease their pain if they are praised for speaking out and believe that their grandparent appreciates how difficult it is for them to be open about what has happened. However hard it might be to bear listening about child abuse, imagine how much more awful it must be to talk about when it has happened to you.

Top Tip: *If your grandchild comes to you and speaks of abuse, 'active listening' is more important than ever.*

A grandchild will also need to be reassured that they are not to blame for the abuse. This might seem an odd statement to make but children, although innocent victims, frequently feel guilty and somehow responsible for what has been done to them. Consequently they need to be convinced that what they have said in no way harms or lessens their grandparents' love. Children can feel dirty, contaminated and unlovable after being abused and so to know that the grandparents' love remains constant and as strong as ever will be a priceless treasure.

 Top Tip: *Abused children need to be reassured that they are not to blame for the abuse.*

During this painful process a grandparent will need to be patient and to exercise judgement. Patience is necessary because the story might be confused and may emerge bit by bit as a child grows in confidence. Judgement will be needed because children, like adults, do sometimes lie, misrepresent events and misunderstand relationships. That said, however, I believe that it is very rare for a grandchild to set out deliberately with the intention of deceiving a grandparent on such a subject. A grandparent should always be prepared to back their own judgement. The emotion shown by grandchildren, the scenes they describe and the words they use will all give a good indication of whether what is said is true or not. Given a grandparent's experience and knowledge, particularly if they have a good relationship with their grandchild, I doubt they are likely to be deceived. I believe it is far, far more likely that a reluctance on the part of the grandparent to believe what is being said will prevent them from understanding their grandchild. There have been cases where, even if they have suspected child abuse, a fear of becoming involved has prevented a grandparent from offering help.

Top Tip: *A situation where abuse is suspected will demand extra reserves of patience, courage and good judgement from a grandparent.*

But that is what an abused grandchild will need – help. Most child abuse occurs in families. Most abusers are people known to the child. This makes intervention hard and especially agonising if the suspected abuser is the grandparents' own child. But if a grandparent believes their grandchild has been, or is being, abused then action *must* follow. Many adults who were abused as children will testify that they tried to get help but were not believed, or were not offered support, for fear that tackling the problem would be too difficult or too painful. A good grandparent will always want to ensure that measures are taken to prevent further abuse and to make their grandchild safe. For this reason grandparents need to be careful not to agree to keep secrets or to promise to respect confidentiality in a way that stops them from taking action. They should tell their grandchild (depending on age and understanding) what will happen next and why. One of the most common complaints from children who have been abused is that once they have spoken out the whole matter is taken out of their hands. They are not consulted, they are not kept informed and often feel that they have lost all control over their own lives.

Top Tip: *However frightening it may seem, grandparents should be always be prepared to take action to prevent abuse or protect a child.*

You Are Not Alone

What action should a grandparent take? It is dangerous to generalise and any action must be specifically geared to the particular circumstances of the grandchild. The following suggestions are no more than examples of the kinds of interventions a grandparent can make. If a grandchild has been abused by someone outside the family then involving the parents might well be the first step. Even if the abuse is within the family getting an innocent partner – father or more likely a mother – to protect the child could be crucial. Research shows that abused children are likely to do better if they continue to have the support of the non-offending parent. A loving barrier needs to be built up of people on the child's side.

Statutory services carry responsibilities for protecting children. If a grandparent fears that their grandchild is in immediate danger they should contact the police. Social services should be involved too. Unfortunately, those two words can strike fear into the hearts of parents and grandparents. This is partly because social services have been heavily criticised in the media in a number of cases. Even so, however, they are the lead agency in this area with a duty to investigate allegations of child abuse, and the bad publicity does not do justice to the many times the involvement of social services has helped to protect a child.

Staff working for social services have a responsibility to put the interests of the child first and they will be committed to serving those interests. Some voluntary agencies can have a part to play too. ChildLine (0800 1111) is always there for a child who wants to seek help or get advice. The NSPCC has a 24-hour freephone helpline (0808 800 5000) for anyone concerned about the wellbeing of a child. If a grandparent is not sure what to do, or wants advice, they can phone this line and speak to a professional with experience in child abuse. Many grandparents do.

 Top Tip: *If your grandchild is in immediate danger, you should contact the police and social services.*

Staying the Distance

Once immediate steps have been taken to make a grandchild safe, a grandparent's involvement should not stop there. Investigations of allegations of child abuse can take a long time and this will be a lengthy period of considerable uncertainty and anxiety for children. They will continue to need persistent and powerful support. If the investigation leads to a criminal case being brought to court it is usual to have, at least, a two-year wait for the trial. Two years is a long time in most of our lives, but in the life of a child it can be an eternity. As grandparents we can play a key role in helping our grand-children to rebuild their confidence and get on with their lives while they wait.

And the trial itself will be an ordeal. Although many measures have been introduced to make it easier for a child to give evidence we are still asking a lot when we expect children to cope with the legal proceedings. I remember attending a legal conference some years ago where a speaker said she would be pointing at random to a few members of the audience and asking them to stand up and describe their latest sexual experience. Along with a roomful of respectable professionals I shrivelled up and tried to make myself invisible. I would have welcomed a granny to hide behind to make sure I was not selected. Of course it did not happen. Having made her point the speaker went on to remind us that we expected children to do far more in cases of child sexual abuse and that they were more vulnerable and helpless, and had endured worse experiences, than any of us in the audience.

I stress the aftermath of child abuse only to underline the importance of continuing support for a grandchild. It can take months for an investigation to be completed, years for a case to come to trial and even longer for a child to try to come to terms with the abuse they have suffered. A tenacious and wise grandparent, uncompromising with their love, can be one of the best companions a child can have on this long, hard road.

 Top Tip: *Children who have been cruelly treated will continue to need the love and companionship of grandparents long after the abuse has stopped.*

Spotting the Signs of Child Abuse

In this chapter we have looked at how grandparents should respond if approached by grandchildren who say they are being abused. But what if the grandchildren cannot tell anybody about what is happening to them, not even their grandparents? Is there anything grandparents can do to recognise child abuse? Or better still, is there any way a grandparent can recognise a grandchild who is at risk and act early enough to prevent child abuse? Prevention is always better than cure and nowhere is this more true than when a child is in danger of being cruelly treated.

A grandparent might be put on guard through their knowledge of what is going on in their grandchild's family or could be alerted because of the nature of their grandchild's relationships. The most likely indication, however, that something is wrong will probably be found in changes in their grandchild's behaviour.

A problem arises because none of the most common behaviour changes on their own, or even in clusters, are proof of child abuse. They might well have other causes and explanations. Nevertheless, the following list, taken from the NSPCC's leaflet, 'Stopping Sexual Abuse Within the Family', may be useful in assisting grandparents to recognise signs that show that their grandchild is in distress.

Sometimes a child who is suffering abuse will show changes in behaviour. He or she may start to:

- avoid being alone with a particular adult;
- show unexpected fear of an adult or be reluctant to socialise with them;
- be unusually clingy;
- behave aggressively or have sleep problems or wet the bed;
- act in a sexually precocious way, including use of sexual language and information not previously known by the child;
- drop hints or clues that suggest abuse. For example, he or she may refer to being asked to keep a secret, or ask questions about Daddy being taken away;
- refuse to attend school or suddenly start performing badly at school;
- appear depressed and withdrawn or complain about physical ailments that don't have a physical explanation.

As grandparents, we should trust our own judgement and, if we are worried, seek professional advice about protecting our grandchild. In many cases of child abuse it is the sound instincts of someone close to a child, coupled with good judgement, that have led to children being rescued from abuse.

Top Tip: *Trust your judgement.*

Although the subject we have been tackling has been child abuse, this chapter also has relevance for children suffering for other reasons. There are many sources of pain for a child but the signs they show will be similar to the ones mentioned here and the need for action remains the same. It would be natural for a grandparent to worry about whether they are doing the right thing if they decide to intervene but, in my experience, it is far more common for people to be reluctant to interfere and to turn aside from a child's plight, than it is for them to exaggerate a child's problems and blunder in blindly. Any action taken sensitively and lovingly with the sole consideration of taking care of the grandchild can be mistaken but it cannot be wrong. What is wrong, if you are concerned, is to do nothing and run the risk of leaving a grandchild abandoned in suffering's cave of darkness.

 Top Tip: If you are truly concerned, the worst thing you can do is nothing at all.

This chapter has dwelled at some length on a painful issue. Consequently a sombre tone has been introduced into grandparenting – a subject that is principally about joy and friendship. However, I think this looking into the shadows is justified for the sake of our most vulnerable children. Child abuse is the most profound wrong children can experience. They need grandparents fighting in the front line to right these wrongs.

ALWAYS RUNNING, JUMPING PLAYING – THOSE GRANDPARENTS OF MINE HAVE ME EXHAUSTED.

Conclusion

In the Heart of a Grandchild

When Grandmama fell off the boat
And couldn't swim (and wouldn't float),
Matilda just stood by and smiled.
I almost could have slapped the child.
          'Indifference', Harry Graham

Fortunately there are not many grandchildren as indifferent as
Matilda and most grandparents, if they cannot swim, are
certainly prepared to float!

During the course of this book we have looked at grandparents at full sail. We have celebrated the many parts they
play and highlighted the significance of the grandparent–child
relationship. We have investigated the way they can add

strength to their families while acknowledging there is no blueprint for being a grandparent. Grandparents have to learn much as they go along but we have considered to what extent they can prepare for their new relationship with their grandchildren. This preparation will be based more on experience and communication than instinct. However, when it arrives, the relationship between a grandparent and grandchild will be one of the most natural relationships in the world.

On this journey through the varied and wonderful world of grandparents, we have examined our roles within the context of the contemporary family and touched on the changes that modern life has brought. An Age Concern survey conducted in 1998 found that very nearly half of today's grandparents felt that the stress of modern life on parents and children is a factor in changing the grandparent–grandchild relationship. Coming to terms with these changes is a must if grandparents are to help parents and children cope with the stresses in their lives.

We saw that being a grandparent involved two relationships, not one: a new relationship with their child turned parent as well as with their grandchild. It is a co-operative relationship with the parent, ensuring responsibilities are shared and consistency achieved on important issues. Sadly this relationship of creative sharing has often been portrayed as one of conflict. Simone de Beauvoir has suggested that 'For old people the affection of the grandchildren is a revenge upon the generation between' (*Old Age*, 1971). It has also been said that the reason grandparents and grandchildren get along so well is because they have a common enemy. If these negative views were true they would result in some very confused grandchildren and a lot of lonely lives of diminishing influence for grandparents.

Top Tip: *Being a grandparent is about two relationships and not one.*

Grandparents, in having very different parts to play, do not have to be in conflict with parents. Instead these differences can be exploited constructively to the advantage of all involved. Grandparents are allowed to be softer and more easy-going than parents can often afford to be, and this is recognised and appreciated by grandchildren. It can be a source of fun and pleasure for them without undermining the parents.

Top Tip: *The relationship between a grandparent and grandchild is one of the most natural relationships in the world.*

I suspect many grandparents aim for the kind of controlled indulgence achieved by the 'fat grandmamma' in Walter de la Mare's 1904 poem, 'The Cupboard':

> I know a little cupboard,
> With a teeny tiny key,
> And there's a jar of lollypops
> For me, me, me.

It has a little shelf, my dear,
As dark, as dark can be,
And there's a dish of Banbury cakes
For me, me, me.

I have a small fat grandmamma,
With a very slippery knee,
And she's keeper of the cupboard
With the key, key, key.

And when I'm very good, my dear,
As good as good can be,
There's Banbury cakes and lollypops
For me, me, me.

On the way, we have looked at more painful subjects and confronted some of the tougher things that can happen to grandchildren, such as the break-up of their parents' marriage, family crises, trauma arising from the stresses of modern life and child abuse. Grandparents can have leading roles to play in helping their grandchildren through these more painful dramas of family life.

 Top Tip: *A good grandparent will be there in the bad times as well as the good times.*

Also on our journey, we noted that while some people are not keen to be grandparents, the wider picture reveals that grandparents generally are becoming increasingly involved with their grandchildren. The Age Concern survey reported that two-thirds of today's grandparents said that they were more involved in the lives of their grandchildren than their parents were with their grandchildren. This involvement can entail providing crucial care for the grandchildren. The same survey disclosed that today's grandparents are more than twice as likely to act as childminders to their grandchildren than the previous generation were.

As well as carers, minders and assistant parents, grandparents are key figures because of the other, varied characters they can be for grandchildren. Grandparents can be:

- warriors, courageous guardians and defenders;
- living ancestors and family historians (grandparents are living time machines);
- teachers, mentors and role models;
- attentive listeners, confidants and best friends;
- uninhibited playmates, wizards and heroes.

As a result of being these many characters, grandparents can offer their grandchildren:

- emotional security, consistency and emotional sanctuary in times of trouble;
- information and skills, especially those lost in modern society;
- a living history and positive image of ageing;
- confidence and self-esteem;
- fun; and
- most of all, love.

The essential ingredients that make grandparents so special are experience, information, knowledge of life, wisdom and a big heart. They are survivors of their own age and can help persuade their grandchildren that they, in turn, will survive the upheavals of this age. The grandparent–grandchild relationship has that delicate balance between loving closeness and the separation that comes through belonging to different generations. Thus it can be passionate and intense and, at the same time, objective and wise.

 Top Tip: Grandparents have so much to offer, but nothing more important than a big heart.

Using Our Resources

Looking outwards at the broader scene we can see how, as a nation, we need to make the most of not only our economic and physical resources but also of our human ones as well. The family, in all its different forms, is at the hub of human relationships, but we need to be able to push beyond the boundaries of the immediate family. Many people are either cut off from being grandparents or, if they are grandparents, feel that they have more to give. The pool of potential grandparents is substantial. At the same time we have many children who are living restricted lives. Nearly all would benefit from having a wider range of relationships with people who could offer love, support and guidance. We should be matching the resources grandparents offer with the needs children have.

Fortunately, there are some good signs and the UK Government is developing a number of initiatives that build on what grandparents can offer. These include encouraging grandparents to go into schools to become mentors to children. This could become part of a nationwide scheme to promote grandparent mentors. Such a scheme would make use of the skills grandparents have but it need not be restricted to schools and nor need it be restricted to the role of mentor. Given the balance of the population there is no reason why every child should not have 'grandparents' playing a variety of roles.

 Top Tip: *Every child should have an active 'grandparent'.*

In the United States of America there is a growing movement that is seeking to apply the wisdom and experience of elders in useful and realistic ways. This will give those people whose grandchildren are out of reach, or those who have no grandchildren of their own, a means of connecting with the young. The formal beginnings of the movement to bring generations closer in the USA came in 1960 when a foster-grandparent programme was launched. Since then many projects have been developed. They have aimed to extend the benefit of the grandparent–grandchild relationship into the community. The results of the movement have included giving grandparents a wider purpose and an increased sense of usefulness. Children have benefited from the extra teaching and guidance they have received in loving and unpressured relationships. Meanwhile, the public at large has become increasingly aware of the advantages of a society that treasures all its members, whatever their age, and breaks down the boundaries between generations.

It's a Two-way Relationship

This book has been written for grandparents and has concentrated on what they have to offer children. I hope, however, that I have made it clear that the relationship between grandparent and grandchild is a two-way relationship. Grandchildren have so much to offer grandparents and all of us who are grandparents will want to give thanks for that. If I give half as much joy to my grandchildren as they give me I will be very grateful.

I have found three aspects of the grandparent–grandchild relationship to have been of special importance for me.

168

The first is the way grandchildren help to keep the child alive within us. Whatever our age, and however impressively mature we might be, we will all have a bit of us that continues to relish the joys of childhood. It is a bit of us that contributes massively to our zest for life. I recognise it in myself, for example, when I am on a beach and I want to paddle, build a sandcastle and eat a melting ice-cream; or when I am in a park and want to slide on the slide, swing on the swing and join in a game of football where coats are used as goalposts; or when I want to read stories about Pooh so that I can meet Piglet, Baby Roo and Eeyore again and bounce like Tigger, play Poohsticks and try to trap a Heffalump; or even when I want to laugh out loud, bounce on the bed or run round the garden for no good reason.

When my children had grown up there were times when I wished I could borrow a child so that I could do something which looked frankly ridiculous when performed by a (supposedly) grown-up man on his own! The arrival of grandchildren releases the constraints and we are free once more.

> Give me a young man in whom there is something of the old, and an old man with something of the young; guided so, a man may grow old in body, but never in mind.
>
> *De Senectute Xi*

Second, grandchildren can connect us to the times in which we live. It is easy enough for us to get stuck and out of touch. How often have you heard people bemoaning that 'It wasn't like this in my day'? 'My day' for these people is the past. 'My day' for our grandchildren is today. Becoming involved with our grandchildren inevitably means becoming involved in what is happening around them. The more we understand the scene the more help we can be. In this process, if we have got lost in times past, being a grandparent can help us discover the relevance of our experience, knowledge and skills to contemporary times. Grandparents have much to offer not only to their families but to their wider communities too. Grandchildren can remind us of our relevance and importance to the world as it is here and now.

Top Tip: *Becoming a grandparent offers the chance of reconnecting with the world as it is here and now.*

Third, grandchildren can help grandparents in their own development. One of the most exciting joys for human beings is that, whatever our age, we never stop developing, changing and growing. Healthy ageing depends on continued change and growth. If we are stuck in our development we can easily become stunted and are unable to achieve our full potential. So while it is good, for example, to remain in touch with the child in us, it is important that we do not get bogged down. We should constantly look to grow and move on. It is a task that can still be absorbing us on our last day. It has been said that the fear of dying is really the fear of not having lived. Grandchildren help us to live our lives to the full. And maybe the last act a grandparent can do for their grandchild is to die well and take the sting out of death.

Top Tip: *Grandchildren help grandparents to live life to the full.*

Building Foundations that Will Last

For all of us, becoming a grandparent is a significant new stage in life. It is another step in our endless seeking of intellectual, emotional, psychological and spiritual maturity. It is a stage that is often characterised by an increasingly selfless approach to life and a lessening of investment in earthly and material things. There is a growing awareness of mortality, a concern for the young and a desire to leave a positive legacy.

Many people have discovered, or rediscovered, self-confidence and self-awareness through forming a positive identity of themselves as grandparents. Grandparents help their grandchildren to grow but grandchildren help their grand-parents continue to grow too.

Looking at what grandparents have contributed in the past and what they are contributing to contemporary life, and listening to the testimony of grandchildren, there is no doubting the importance of grandparents. However, all this mass of material, and all the contributions to be made and all the parts to be played, must not be allowed to obscure the fact that being a grandparent is a blessing. It is great fun. It is a pure joy. According to Hannah Whitall Smith, 'If becoming a grandparent was only a matter of choice I should advise everyone of you straight away to become one. There is no fun for old people like

171

it!' (quoted in *Philadelphia Quaker*, Logan Pearsall Smith, 1978).

Nor amid all that grandparents can do should we ever underestimate the importance of them simply 'being there' – a constant loving feature of a grandchild's life.

> **Top Tip:** *The importance of simply being there for our grandchildren should never be underestimated.*

The Last Word Is Love

After all the words and all the chapters, after all the subjects and all the issues that have been covered in this book, we are left with the most important word of all – love. That is the most precious gift any of us as grandparents can give to our grandchildren. It will surely be returned. There is more than enough darkness, hatred and violence in the world but I agree with Martin Luther King who proclaimed love to be the most durable power in the world. That durable power is to be found in its most indomitable form in the relationship between a grandparent and a grandchild.

And so, how do we grandparents know how we are doing? How do we know what kind of job we are doing as grandparents? There are no examinations, no impartial assessments and no targets. And thank goodness for that. At the end of the day the only worthwhile measure of us as grandparents lies within the heart of our grandchild.

Further Information

Organisations

Parentalk
PO Box 23142
London SE1 0ZT

Tel: 0700 2000 500
Fax: 020 7450 9060
e-mail: info@parentalk.co.uk
Web site: www.parentalk.co.uk

Provides a range of resources and services designed to inspire parents to enjoy parenthood.

Parentalk at Work
Web site:
   www.parentalkatwork.co.uk

A new arm of Parentalk, aimed specifically at helping parents strike a healthy work–life balance.

Care for the Family
PO Box 488
Cardiff CF15 7YY

Tel: 029 2081 0800
Fax: 029 2081 4089
e-mail:
   care.for.the.family@cff.org.uk
Web site:
   www.care-for-the-family.org.uk

Provides support for families through seminars, resources and special projects.

Child Benefit Centre
Waterview Park
Pattenson Industrial Estate
Washington
Tyne and Wear NE38 8QA

Tel: 08701 555540
e-mail:
  childbenefit@mso4.dss.gov.uk
Web site: www.dss.gov.uk

Administers all child benefit claims.

Child Support Agency
PO Box 55
Brierley Hill
West Midlands DY5 1YL
Tel: 08457 133133 (enquiry line)

In Northern Ireland:
Great Northern Tower
17 Great Victoria Street
Belfast BT2 7AD
Tel: 028 9089 6896

The Government agency that ass-esses maintenance levels for parents who no longer live with their children.

Children 1st
41 Polwarth Terrace
Edinburgh EH11 1NU

Tel: 0131 337 8539
Fax: 0131 346 8284
e-mail: children1st@zetnet.co.uk

A national Scottish voluntary organisation providing advice and support to parents on the care and protection of their children.

Citizens' Advice Bureau (CAB)
Web site: www.nacab.org.uk

A free and confidential service giving information and advice on benefits, maternity rights, debt, housing, consumer, employment and legal problems as well as family and personal difficulties. Ask at your local library or look in your phone book for your nearest office.

Contact-A-Family
209–211 City Road
London EC1V 1JN

Helpline: 0808 808 3555
Tel: 020 7608 8700
Fax: 020 7608 8701
e-mail: info@cafamily.org.uk
Web site: www.cafamily.org.uk

Brings together families whose children have disabilities.

Council for Disabled Children
8 Wakley Street
London EC1V 7QE

Tel: 020 7843 6061/6058
Fax: 020 7278 9512
e-mail: jkhan@ncb.org.uk
Web site: www.ncb.org.uk

Provides an information and advice service on all matters relating to disability for children and their families.

Dads & Lads
YMCA England National Dads &
  Lads Project
Dee Bridge House
25–27 Lower Bridge Street
Chester CH1 1RS

Tel: 01244 403090
e-mail: dirk@parenting.ymca.org.uk
      ahowie@themail.co.uk

*Locally based projects run jointly by
YMCA and Care for the Family for
fathers and sons, mentors and boys.
They offer a unique opportunity to
get together with other fathers and
sons for a game of football and
other activities. To find out where
your nearest Dads & Lads project
is based or to get help starting a new
one, please contact Dirk Uitterdijk
at the above address.*

**Department for Work and Pensions (formerly the
Department of Social Security)**
Tel: 020 712 2171
Web site: www.dss.gov.uk

In Northern Ireland:
Castle Buildings
Stormont Estate
Upper Newtownards Road
Belfast BT4 3SG
Tel: 028 9052 0500

*Gives general advice on all social
security benefits, pensions and
National Insurance, including maternity benefits and income support.*

Disabled Parents' Network
Helpline: 0870 241 0450
e-mail: information@disabled
    parentsnetwork.org.uk
Web site: www.disabledparents
    network.org.uk

*A support network run by disabled
parents for disabled people thinking
about becoming parents, pregnant
disabled people and disabled
parents.*

Down's Syndrome Association
In England:
155 Mitcham Road
London SW17 9PG
Tel: 020 8682 4001 (Tues–Thurs
    10 a.m.–4 p.m.)

In Northern Ireland:
Graham House
Knockenbracken Healthcare Park
Saintfield Road
Belfast BT8 8BH
Tel: 028 9070 4606

In Wales:
206 Whitchurch Road
Cardiff CF14 3NB
Tel: 029 2052 2511

UK web site:
  www.dsa-uk.com

Family Service Units
207 Old Marylebone Road
London NW1 5QP

Tel: 020 7402 5175
Fax: 020 7724 1829
e-mail: centraloffice@fsu.org.uk
Web site: www.fsu.org.uk

*Units across the country provide
support and advice for families with
problems.*

Fathers Direct
Tamarisk House
37 The Tele Village
Crickhowell
Powys NP8 1BP

Tel: 01873 810515
Web site: www.fathersdirect.com

An information resource for fathers.

Gingerbread
16–17 Clerkenwell Close
London EC1R 0AA

Tel: 020 7336 8183
Fax: 020 7336 8185
e-mail: office@gingerbread.org.uk
Web site: www.gingerbread.org.uk

*Provides day-to-day support and
practical help for lone parents.*

Grandparents Federation
Moot House
The Stow
Harlow
Essex CM20 3AG

Advice line: 01279 444964
Tel: 01279 428040
e-mail: grandfed@talk21.com
Web site: www.grandparents-
federation.org.uk

*Offers advice and support for
grandparents.*

Health Development Agency
30 Great Peter Street
London SW1P 2HW

Publications: 01235 465565
Tel: 020 7222 5300
Fax: 020 7413 8900
Web site: www.hda-online.org.uk

*Produces a wide range of leaflets
and other useful information on a
variety of topics for families.*

Home-Start UK
2 Salisbury Road
Leicester LE1 7QR
Tel: 0116 233 9955
Fax: 0116 233 0232
e mail: info@home-start.org.uk
Web site: www.home-start.org.uk

In Northern Ireland:
133 Bloomfield Avenue
Belfast BT5
Tel/fax: 028 9046 0772

Volunteers offer support, friendship and practical help to young families in their own homes.

Meningitis Trust
Fern House
Bath Road
Stroud
Gloucestershire GL5 3TJ

Tel: 0808 800 3344
Web site:
www.meningitis-trust.org.uk

Supplies facts about meningitis and septicaemia and details of specific research.

Mind (National Association for Mental Health)
Granta House
15–19 Broadway
London E15 4BQ

Helpline: 020 8522 1728/0345 660 163 (Mon, Wed & Thur 9.15 a.m.–4.45 p.m.)
Tel: 020 8519 2122
Fax: 020 8522 1725
e-mail: contact@mind.org.uk
Web site: www.mind.org.uk

Has over 200 branches across England and Wales, most of which offer counselling services for individuals suffering from depression and other mental health problems. Mind's helpline offers advice and support.

National Association for People Abused in Childhood (NAPAC)
42 Curtain Road
London EC2A 3NH

NAPAC exists to assist adults who have experienced neglect or ill-treatment in childhood.

National Asthma Campaign
Providence House
Providence Place
London N1 0NT

Helpline: 0845 701 0203 (run by nurses 9 a.m.–7 p.m.)
Tel: 020 7266 2260
Web site: www.asthma.org.uk

The National Asthma Campaign is the independent UK charity working to conquer asthma, in partnership with people with asthma and all who share their concern, through a combination of research, education and support.

The National Autistic Society
393 City Road
London EC1V 1NG

Autism helpline: 020 7903 3555 (Mon–Fri 10 a.m.–4 p.m.)
Parent to Parent: 0800 9520 520 (your call is logged on an answer phone and the relevant regional volunteer calls you back)
Tel: 0870 600 8585
e-mail: autismhelpline@nas.org.uk
Web site: www.oneworld.org/autism-uk

National Childminding Association
8 Masons Hill
Bromley
Kent BR2 9EY

Advice line: 0800 169 4486 (Mon, Tues & Thurs 10 a.m.–12 & 2–4 p.m.; Fri 2–4 p.m.)
Tel: 020 8464 6164
Fax: 020 8290 6834
e-mail: info@ncma.org.uk
Web site: www.ncma.org.uk

Informs childminders, parents and employers about the best practice in childminding.

National Council for One Parent Families
255 Kentish Town Road
London NW5 2LX

Lone Parent Line: 0800 018 5026
Maintenance & Money Line: 020 7428 5424 (Mon & Fri 10.30 a.m.–1.30 p.m.; Wed 3–6 p.m.)
Web site:
www.oneparentfamilies.org.uk

An information service for lone parents.

National Eczema Society
Hill House
Highgate Hill
London N19 5NA

Information line: 0870 241 3604 (weekdays 1–4 p.m.)
General enquiries: 020 7281 3553
Web site: www.eczema.org

The National Eczema Society is the only charity in the UK dedicated to providing support and information for people with eczema and their carers.

National Family and Parenting Institute
430 Highgate Studios
53–79 Highgate Road
London NW5 1TL

Tel: 020 7424 3460
Fax: 020 7485 3590
e-mail: info@nfpi.org
Web site: www.nfpi.org

An independent charity set up to provide a strong national focus on parenting and families in the twenty-first century.

National NEWPIN (New Parent and Infant Network)
Sutherland House
35 Sutherland Square
Walworth
London SE17 3EE

Tel: 020 7703 6326
Fax: 020 7701 2660
e-mail: quality@nationalnewpin.freeserve.co.uk
Web site: www.newpin.org.uk

A network of local centres offering a range of services for parents and children.

NHS Direct
Advice line: 0845 4647
Web site: www.nhsdirect.co.uk

NHS Smoking Quitline
Helpline: 0800 169 0169
Web site:
   www.giveupsmoking.co.uk

NIPPA (The early years organisation)
6C Wildflower Way
Belfast BT12 6TA

Tel: 028 9066 2825
Fax: 028 9038 1270
e-mail: mail@nippa.org
Web site: www.nippa.org

Promotes high-quality early childhood care and education services.

NSPCC
NSPCC National Centre
42 Curtain Road
London EC2A 3NH

Helpline: 0800 800 5000
Tel: 020 7825 2500
Fax: 020 7825 2525
Web site: www.nspcc.org.uk

Aims to prevent child abuse and neglect in all its forms and give practical help to families with children at risk. The NSPCC also produces leaflets with information and advice on positive parenting – for these, call 020 7825 2500.

One Parent Families Scotland
13 Gayfield Square
Edinburgh EH1 3NX

Tel: 0131 556 3899/4563
Fax: 0131 557 9650
e-mail: opfs@gn.apc.org

Web site: www.gn.apc.org/opfs

Provides information, training, counselling and support to one-parent families throughout Scotland.

Parenting Education & Support Forum
Unit 431 Highgate Studios
53–79 Highgate Road
London NW5 1TL

Tel: 020 7284 8370
Fax: 020 7485 3587
e-mail: pesf@dial.pipex.com
Web site:
   www.parenting-forum.org.uk

Aims to raise awareness of the importance of parenting and its impact on all aspects of child development.

Parentline Plus
520 Highgate Studios
53–76 Highgate Road
Kentish Town
London NW5 1TL

Helpline: 0808 800 2222
Textphone: 0800 783 6783
Fax: 020 7284 5501
e-mail: centraloffice@parentline
   plus.org.uk
Web site:
   www.parentlineplus.org.uk

Provides a freephone helpline called Parentline and courses for parents via the Parent Network Service. Parentline Plus also includes the National Stepfamily Association. For all information, call the Parentline freephone number: 0808 800 2222.

Parents Advice Centre
Floor 4
Franklin House
12 Brunswick Street
Belfast BT2 7GE

Helpline: 028 9023 8800
e-mail: belfast@pachelp.org
Web site:
    www.parentsadvicecentre.org

Parents Anonymous
6–9 Manor Gardens
London N7 6LA

Tel: 020 7263 8918 (Mon–Fri)

24-hour answering service for parents who feel they can't cope or feel they might abuse their children.

Parents at Work
45 Beech Street
London EC2Y 8AD

Tel: 020 7628 3565
Fax: 020 7628 3591
e-mail: info@parentsatwork.org.uk
Web site:
    www.parentsatwork.org.uk

Provides advice and information about childcare provision.

Positive Parenting
1st Floor
2A South Street
Gosport PO12 1ES

Tel: 023 9252 8787
Fax: 023 9250 1111
e-mail: info@parenting.org.uk

Web site: www.parenting.org.uk

Aims to prepare people for the role of parenting by helping parents, those about to become parents and also those who lead parenting groups.

Principal Registry of the Family Division
First Avenue House
42–49 High Holborn
London WC1V 6NP

Children section: 020 7947 6936
Web site: www.courtservice.gov.uk

Relate
Herbert Gray College
Little Church Street
Rugby CV21 3AP
Tel: 01788 573241
e-mail:
    enquiries@national.relate.org.uk
Web site: www.relate.org.uk

In Northern Ireland:
76 Dublin Road
Belfast BT2 7HP
Tel: 028 9032 3454

Provides a confidential counselling service for relationship problems of any kind. Local branches are listed in the phone book.

Publications

The Children Act – What's in it for grandparents? (Grandparents Federation)
Looking After Your Grandchild (Grandparents Federation)

Parenting Courses

- **Parentalk Parenting Course**
  A new parenting course designed to give parents the opportunity to share their experiences, learn from each other and discover some principles of parenting. For more information, phone 0700 2000 500.

- **Positive Parenting**
  Publishes a range of low-cost, easy-to-read, common-sense resource materials which provide help, information and advice. Responsible for running a range of parenting courses across the UK. For more information, phone 023 9252 8787.

- **Parent Network**
  For more information, call Parentline Plus on 0808 800 2222.

The **Paren**talk Parenting Course

Helping you to be a Better Parent

Being a parent is not easy. **Parentalk** is a new, video-led, parenting course designed to give groups of parents the opportunity to share their experiences, learn from each other and discover some principles of parenting. It is suitable for anyone who is a parent or is planning to become a parent.

The Parentalk Parenting Course features:

Steve Chalke – TV Presenter; author on parenting and family issues; father of four and **Parentalk** Chairman.
Rob Parsons – author of *The Sixty Minute Father* and *The Sixty Minute Mother*; and Executive Director of Care for the Family.
Dr Caroline Dickinson – inner city-based GP and specialist in obstetrics, gynaecology and paediatrics.
Kate Robbins – well-known actress and comedienne.

Each **Parentalk** session is packed with group activities and discussion starters.

Made up of eight sessions, the **Parentalk** Parenting Course is easy to use and includes everything you need to host a group of up to ten parents.

Each Parentalk Course Pack contains:
- A **Parentalk** video
- Extensive, easy-to-use, group leader's guide
- Ten copies of the full-colour course material for members
- Photocopiable sheets/OHP masters

Price £49.95

Additional participant materials are available so that the course can be run again and again.

To order your copy, or to find out more, please contact:

Parentalk
PO Box 23142, London SE1 0ZT
Tel: 0700 2000 500
Fax: 020 7450 9060
e-mail: info@parentalk.co.uk